Rita,

This book is so very outstanding in the fact that JoAnn gives credence to the difficulties that we face, as she did + does also. As we read of her struggles in life-style, through illness, it her strength gives strength to us in our changes, as well.

The "Joy" in her journey is the final acceptance of these changes and being able to enjoy life in her limitations.

I pray for you through your many struggles — especially through your present surgery and your Chronic Fatigue Syndrome.

We are "soul-sisters", as well as being dear friends in our struggles of limitations in life-style.

Share this with others who also face our similar experiences. That was how I learned of this book. This will be reviewed and discussed at the Baptist Women's Round Table (Book Club) in August of this year — 1997.

My love and prayers,
Jane Milligan Berger

Fellow-Savannahian!

JOY IN THE JOURNEY

JOY
IN THE
JOURNEY

Jo Ann Paris Leavell

Foreword by
Rhonda Harrington Kelley

PELICAN PUBLISHING COMPANY
Gretna 1994

The word "Pelican" and the depiction of a pelican are trademarks of Pelican Publishing Company, Inc., and are registered in the U.S. Patent and Trademark Office.

Library of Congress Cataloging-in-Publication Data

Leavell, Jo Ann Paris.
   Joy in the journey / Jo Ann Paris Leavell ; foreword by Rhonda
Harrington Kelley.
     p. cm.
   ISBN 1-56554-021-2
   1. Leavell, Jo Ann Paris. 2. Baptists—United States—Biography.
3. Cerebrovascular disease—Patients—Biography. 4. Cerebrovascular
disease—Religious aspects—Christianity. I. Title.
BX6495.L37A3 1994
286'.1'092—dc20
[B]   93-47619
                                            CIP

Manufactured in the United States of America
Published by Pelican Publishing Company, Inc.
1101 Monroe Street, Gretna, Louisiana 70053

TO MY EIGHT GRANDCHILDREN:

Virginia Gentry Leavell (Gentry)
Jo Ann Paris Leavell (Paris)

Finis Leavell Beauchamp (Beau)
Andrew Leavell Beauchamp (Andrew)
Jo Ann Leavell Beauchamp (Jo Ann)
David Leavell Beauchamp (David)

Lucy Ann Leavell (Lucy)
Roland Quinche Leavell III (Ro)

*I'm not rich and famous . . .
but I do have priceless grandchildren
who truly are life's dessert!*

Joy in the Journey

Along with friends and family
We travel up the road—
A happy band of pilgrims, heaven is our goal.
And we love this life we're living,
Discovering each day
That the joys of the journey are many on the way.

Now we're moving with a purpose,
An eternal point of view.
Like the years that hurry by us,
We're only passing through.
Now we work for Jesus gladly to give our best away,
Satisfied in knowing our labor's not in vain.

Chorus:
   Joy in the journey—good times in the going.
   It's not all in the reaping;
   There's plenty in the sowing.
   Taking pleasure in the progress
     we make from day to day;
   Joy in the journey to heaven all the way.

Well it's true there are some struggles
And sure there are some tears
But they're so outweighed by blessing
They just fade and disappear.
Now we're helping one another
As to higher ground we climb
And the light on the horizon
Gets brighter all the time.

Contents

Foreword

Since 1975 Jo Ann Leavell has been a personal friend and encourager along my journey in life and ministry. Her positive spirit, delightful charm, and open communication have been examples for me and many others. Her journey through life has been rich with family heritage and Christian service. While her life has not always been easy, it has always been good. The joy in her journey is contagious! I am so grateful for the precious testimony of my mentor and friend, Jo Ann Leavell.

In her book *Joy in the Journey*, Jo Ann explores the challenges of her recent illness and the promises of God's Word, which encourage all who face the valleys of life. Her example of triumph over depression will help all Christians seek true joy in every circumstance. She also offers valuable advice to guide us in helping our friends. *Joy in the Journey* is filled with personal stories, biblical promises, and helpful hints for all who travel life's journey.

For those in the valley of despair, *Joy in the Journey* will bring you hope and help. For those who are at this moment on the mountaintop, the book will multiply your joy. For all of us this inspiring book will suggest many ways to encourage others. Whether in the valley or on the mountaintop, Jo Ann Leavell assures us of God's strength and provision. There can be joy in any journey as believers trust Him!

RHONDA HARRINGTON KELLEY

Acknowledgments

I gratefully express appreciation to the many people who have encouraged me to write another book and who have suggested that something I have written may have helped them.

I owe an unpayable debt of gratitude to Teresa Rhyne, who typed the bulk of this manuscript and offered many helpful suggestions and corrections.

My deepest thanks go to Carol Corvin and Retia Dukes, whose friendship, constant help, and encouragement were invaluable.

My undying love goes to my husband and children, who challenged and encouraged me along the way. They supported me through my constant fear of failure and helped me believe I had something to offer.

Nina Kooij is an able editor whose skill I admire and whose disposition makes working with her a joy.

Nancy and Milburn Calhoun at Pelican Publishing Company have been friends for most of my journey. Nancy and I were high-school and college friends, and I would not have dared to call myself a writer had they not given me a large "push."

Heartfelt thanks go to the many friends who never missed an opportunity to bolster my confidence through clippings, handwritten notes, tidbits from church bulletins, poems, and other materials. This has made it difficult to locate the author and copyright ownership of some of the material. However, I'm indebted to these writers, whose works literally kept me going during my desert experience.

And far from least is Rhonda Kelley, my working partner, who wrote the foreword and helped immeasurably with the study questions.

Introduction

Well, here I go again writing a book. When I wrote *Don't Miss the Blessing* (Pelican Publishing Company, 1990), I vowed that was it! I had protested to the Lord all through the writing of it and declared that was alpha and omega. Never did I plan to do that again!

In fact, I'm still arguing with the Lord about the wisdom of a second book. Why me? Why not others who have had experiences far more traumatic than mine? Why not someone more gifted in literary style and vocabulary? Why write a second book when the first one is not selling? In 1990 because of circumstances beyond my control that I'll mention later, I had to "get off the road." As with an evangelist, when you don't speak and people don't know you, they don't buy your book.

Needless to say, the answer to those questions is not material. It is strictly *obedience*. In the first chapter of Revelation John was told to *write down* his vision. I'm sure John didn't understand "why" any more than I do about the compulsion I feel to write another book. John had no choice if he was going to be faithful, nor do I. Believe me, that is my only motive—*obedience*.

I've just been through the worst time of my life, and I think I have learned the wisdom of "writing it down." Why? Because otherwise we are so prone to forget. We forget God's goodness in the past, we forget promises made, we forget lessons learned, and maybe we even forget how we felt at a particular time.

During my recent illness I kept a journal for the first time in my life. It was a journal kept by a weary person through a desolate wilderness experience. Little did I know at the time it would eventually be a book. Sharing personal experiences is never easy because most of us shy away from being so transparent. I agree with Tim Hansel who said, "Sharing personal journals is a bit like opening one's underwear drawer in public." However, I'm going to risk it, and my prayer is that this book may speak to you in your hour of need, as we are "fellow sufferers."

JOY IN THE JOURNEY

CHAPTER 1

Journey in the Valley

THE EXCITING THING about living with Landrum Leavell is that it is never dull. There are always surprises. The title of this book is one of those little serendipities, as we would say in Louisiana.

We were riding along in the car as we often do listening to tapes of gospel music. This particular day the tape was a new one given to him by a friend. There was a catchy little melody on it entitled, "Joy in the Journey." Landrum looked over at me and said, "Mom, that would be a good title for your next book!" I nearly fainted because the ink was barely dry on the first one.

As I look back, I'm confident the seed was planted right then for this book to be germinated in the "fullness of time." Little did I know the circuitous route the Lord was going to take to prepare me for sharing "my journey." I guess my writings could be called "experiential." The road has not been an easy one, but *joy* has never been far behind.

I have just been through the worst time of my life! It is amazing how one day can change *everything*. On October 27, 1990 everything in my life changed. I had been asked to do a women's conference meeting at the Embassy Suites Hotel in Baton Rouge, Louisiana. It was to begin Friday night concluding Saturday noon. The girls were all excited about this weekend break—staying away for an evening from all family responsibilities. Saturday morning we were to have two more sessions with a break in between before going home. The neat thing about it was that my married daughter, who lived in Baton Rouge at the time, had been asked to be my roommate. As most of you mothers know, that was to be a rare privilege. I had looked forward to this particular conference for a long time and was excited. Well, I spoke to the Friday-night session, went to Shoney's with a group for fellowship, and had a wonderful evening.

The dual morning session was to begin at nine o'clock. I was to speak both times with a break in between. As I recount this experience, I want you to listen carefully for God's provision for me. I came to the platform, laid my notes on the podium as I always do, but there was one difference. I realized my hand was not "working." My right hand was numb from about the elbow down. Thinking *surely* it must be just asleep, I massaged it as I continued to talk. Women often think talk cures everything! You can't imagine what goes through your mind when you are before a group who is expecting you to produce, and it is becoming increasingly difficult even to concentrate. My only daughter, Ann, said, "Mama, the first words you spoke were: 'Something up here is dead.'" She thought I was talking about the PA system! When I realized something truly was wrong, I had to swallow pride and admit I had a problem. At that point, I had no idea what it was—only that my feelings were not normal.

My friend Ginny Foster, who was in charge of the conference, used amazing poise in this difficult situation. She put her hand on my shoulder and said, "Let's pray." I want you to know she prayed the stars down! I was completely aware of everything going on as she prayed for me, my daughter who was by that time at my feet, the girls, the conference, and for God's will to be done. When she concluded, someone remembered seeing a doctor in the coffee shop. As Providence would have it, he was still there. He took my pulse, looked in my eyes, and said, "I don't see anything, but if you keep having trouble, I would go to the emergency room and have it checked out."

Another of God's provisions for me was that I had with me a handout on "friends." The reason I knew it was of the Lord was that it was not my normal habit to carry around a lot of paperwork. Ginny had told me that the Sunday after the retreat was to be "bring-a-friend Sunday" in their church. She said I might want to say something about friends during the conference, so I had planned to talk in one session about friends and friendships. It was most unusual for me to have prepared a work sheet. Ann and I had even talked about how to use it in my presentation. I was undecided about the use of that material, but God in His providential care wasn't. As I left for the emergency room, I said to the group, "Here, you look up the Scriptures on this sheet. I will be back by the time you go in the second session, and we will discuss it." Needless to say, I was not to come back. I heard later they looked up those Scriptures, had their break, and came back for discussion in the second session. I promise you they got a lot more out of that conference than if I had been there. God really did provide.

Ann knew the location of the nearest hospital in Baton Rouge. This was provision number four. As it turned out I stayed three days, and had every test known to man. When the doctor came in the last day, he said, "Mrs. Leavell, we think you have had a light stroke." I said, "Look, you don't understand, I don't have strokes!" I guess I thought it was not in the realm of possibility for me to have a stroke. Ann finally said to me, "Mama, you can't even say that word, can you?" I said, "No." They kidded me later because I kept calling it a little "episode." Now there is a family joke about my little "episode."

You see I had always operated *wide open. Nothing* slowed me down. I have always had lots of energy. I've never felt bad; I never even take a Bufferin. In my mind I had thought of taking care of everybody in the family, but never entertained the possibility anything could happen to *me*. I don't know whether you are like that or not. Let me tell you, *it can happen to you!*

I returned to New Orleans still in shock from this sudden change in events. My gynecologist, who was my only contact with the medical profession, had just retired. Due to my good health, the need had never arisen for any other care. Again pride entered in. I had to face a new doctor who did not know my life-style, my former pace, that I was *not* a hypochondriac. That just *killed* me.

For six months I went through tests. If you are not sick when you go to the doctor, you will be sick when you leave! Once again, I had every test known to man, and most of them twice. I had two MRIs (magnetic resonance imaging). This is a diagnostic machine that generates images of the inside of the body. I wore the heart monitor twice, had an angiogram, seven EEGs (electroencephalograms), EKGs (electrokymograms), stress tests, and numerous other tests. In the process I found out a lot I *didn't* have, but the doctors seemed unable to pin down my problem. The EEG was the only test that showed any irregularity. The doctor said the test was normal, but on the edge of normal. My kids said, "Mama, we have known that all along! We could have told you and saved you lots of money." I don't know what I would have done without a little humor along the way.

To make a long story short, every test I had in Baton Rouge was repeated at least once. You can imagine what that did to my nerves. I was about *shot*. In that period of six months, I saw seven doctors. Exactly five months to the day after my "episode," on March 27, the doctors concluded I *did* have a light stroke. My middle son, Roland, said to me on the telephone, "Mama, you have got to learn to say the 's' word. Now, say it. 'S-t-r-o-k-e.'" I felt like a child. It was as if it was a dirty word. I am so grateful there was no residual impairment.

As I look back, I had not to that point been immune to pain and suffering. My children were all born by Caesarean section. I have had four breast biopsies, a hysterectomy, and other lesser maladies.

But I want you to know that when they start talking about the brain, it is a whole different ball game. For one thing, I don't understand about the brain. I didn't know what was happening, and no one bothered to explain anything to me to lessen my apprehension.

This was a rough year. In fact, it was an awesome year and one I don't care ever to repeat. I have had to apologize to the Lord and to a lot of people for my former attitude. You see, I had never had any patience with people who did not feel good. I had always thought if you didn't feel good, just get up and *do* something. Just snap your fingers, quit thinking about it, and you would be all right.

I have found there are some things that can't be cured simply by a positive attitude. I found out the hard way it is not that simple. You can't always conjure up energy by just "doing things." Problems don't always go away with the snap of your fingers.

I came to the point where I could barely function. It was an effort to get a meal on the table. The things I had always loved— like hospitality, entertaining, teaching—I could no longer do. I had to cancel six or seven months of speaking engagements. I have never had to cancel anything in my life. That was *no* fun, plus it hurt my pride again.

JOURNAL ENTRY

Landrum called Barbara O'Chester and canceled my last engagement for the summer. I hope I did right. It is amazing how quickly a smooth, controlled existence can turn into a catastrophe—how quickly those of us who are strong can become weak. Help me to understand that You allow the storms to strengthen us—not to shipwreck us.

It is *hard* for those of us who are strong to admit a weakness. We pride ourselves in "having things under control." It was hard to admit my control was "out of control," but I had to do it. You know what I found? The world did not cave in or stop when I had to cancel. Those engagements were filled with people who probably did a much better job. It was a year in which I feel I learned a lot.

Following that initial experience the doctors advised me to slow down, take things easier, and learn to "smell the roses." I came home from the hospital on Tuesday and was supposed to teach my last Bible study of the fall on Thursday. Landrum asked me who was going to teach that day. I said, "I am." He said, "Oh no you aren't." I said, "Well, you'd better start studying Philippians then!" He did—and I began the process that is still going on of trying to change an addictive life-style.

It has been said that workaholics are as hard to cure as alcoholics. The bad thing was I didn't *want* to change. I *like* my lifestyle. My children had been telling me for years, "Mama, you and Daddy need to slow down." My response was always, "Why? I *like* the fast lane. Why stop what you enjoy?"

As I look back, I realize it took a *major* blowout to get my attention. I had been having some voice problems for six years. My family insisted I go to the doctor, and after a series of tests the only conclusion seemed to be stress. At that time I hardly believed there was such a thing, and certainly not for *me*. I insisted I was *not* a stressful person, and whatever my voice problems were, they certainly were not due to stress!

Isn't it amazing how sure we can be and be so wrong? I continue to be plagued by voice problems, and yes, they obviously are from stress. Had I not been so strongheaded years ago, who knows if perhaps this could have been avoided. I'm amazed at the patience the Lord has with us "slow learners." I go back to the verse in Prov.

3:12, "For whom the Lord loveth He correcteth . . . ," and though I have become weary of His correction at times, I'm grateful for His tough love.

The stress from all of these problems caused an additional problem. The testing revealed a mitral valve prolapse condition. I'm told this is a common malady affecting approximately 35 percent of people, the majority of them women. It is *not* life threatening, but it *is* life-style threatening. I did not want to hear that. It is a thickening of a heart valve that causes it not to open and close properly. What the doctors think happened in my case is that a microscopic clot from the thickening of that valve sloughed off and went to the brain. The doctor said, "Mrs. Leavell, it could have gone to any other part of your body, and you probably would never have known it." Obviously it is a rare thing and something not likely ever to happen again.

However, I did not want to hear the words "life-style threatening." A change in life-style for me was the loss of a part of my life, a part of my essential being. I did not like to hear about anything that was going to mess up what I enjoyed so well. I kept telling the Lord, "Now, Lord, You have given me a love for Your work, a love for teaching Your truths. Now please don't take it away." I wanted a quick fix—"just give me a pill!" I have reached the place after all these months that if He takes it all away, that is okay, too. You see, He does not owe me an explanation. What I want you to understand is, I would have gone *under* without my faith. I called upon every Scripture I had ever known. I called upon every principle I had ever taught. I hung onto everything I had ever known about the Lord. If you don't have anything to call upon when the storms come, you are going to be in *big* trouble. James said it is not a case of "if" trials come, it is "when" they come.

Nobody told me you fell apart at fifty-nine! If you are not there yet, just pass over that year. It is not a good one. Remember that *you don't get ready for a crisis while you're having one.* You don't prepare for tragedy during the tragedy. You do in an emergency what you have been doing prior to the emergency. If I had not known anything about the Lord and His ways and His truths, at that point I don't believe I would have been rational enough to have known where to go. I have been so grateful that I at least knew where to turn, that I knew Him and where to take my questions of faith. You must have *your* faith and some "holy habits." Some of us "traffic in unpracticed truth"—a very dangerous practice for any Christian to do!

As Chuck Swindoll wrote, "You can't warm by anyone else's fire!" "Behold, all ye that kindle a fire . . . walk in the light of *your* fire, and in the sparks that *ye* have kindled . . ." (Isa. 50:11). We have to gather the driftwood daily that will light the winter fire!

This is the best definition of a crisis I've seen: "A crisis is any set of circumstances which threatens a person's sense of well-being or interferes with his/her normal routine." Believe me, my well-being was threatened and my normal routine was *shot.* I could barely function. Crises come in all kinds of shapes and sizes. They can be economic crises, health crises, financial crises, marriage problems, or a problem with a child—anything too big for us to handle on our own. They are going to come at some point in our lives, and our job is simply to trust and to be as ready as possible for those times.

Heroes have been described as those who are present and respond in crisis situations. Such a one is faithful where he serves and is ready when a crisis breaks out. I pray you will be "ready" for the inevitable crises of life.

I saw one of our seminary professors on campus at about my lowest point, and he said, "Jo Ann, how are you doing?" I said, "Well, I'm hanging in there." He said, "Anybody who ever tells you 'walking by faith' is easy just hasn't been there. It is a lot easier to preach about faith than it is to practice it." Because of problems in his life, I knew he was speaking from experience. It is one thing to preach a sermon, another to live a life. It is easier to read it in a book than walk it in the land, but the walking is what gives us credibility. Just remember, "a rose is crushed before it is fragrant and the finest fruit may be among the thorns!"

PRAYER

Lord, I know You have some hidden purpose in my pain. I don't know where You are going, but I do know You are going with me. Give me the assurance that every step I take in the journey is in Your company.

Questions for Chapter 1

1) Think back on your own life. What valley experiences have you faced? How did God use them to strengthen you?

2) Has the Lord ever had to slow you down in order to speak to you? What did you learn during that time?

3) Carefully study Prov. 3:12. In what ways has God had to correct you?

CHAPTER 2

Joy in the Journey

I REMEMBER SPEAKING at a woman's conference in First Baptist Church, Orlando on the theme, "Certain in an Uncertain World." This was five months into the Persian Gulf War, yet this theme had been chosen well before that conflict. Can you imagine a subject any more relevant or a planning committee with any greater insight and wisdom?

My preparation for that special weekend probably proved to be of far greater value to me than it was to those who attended. As I looked back over my life and experiences, I came to renewed convictions about the certainties of my life—those things about which I am *sure*. The first of these is the assurance the Lord is going to guide me in this endeavor. I guess it is a source of worry for all of us that we will not meet life's most challenging moments. I have agonized over writing this book. I have sensed my inadequacies, but I *know* the Lord is going to see me through. I not only feel He has given me something to say, but He is going to give me the ability to share it with you. This assurance comes from Scripture: "Do not worry about what to say or how to say it. At that time you will be given what to say, for it will not be you speaking, but the Spirit of your Father speaking through you" (Matt. 10:19-20 NIV®).

My only task and yours is to open our minds in calm assurance for a wisdom beyond ourselves. We were never meant to be adequate on our own. The Holy Spirit will strengthen us for our responsibilities. He speaks to us and through us. I am praying even now, "Lord, speak to me that I might write it down." If there is anything I want more than anything else in this world it is to share my faith, but always in His timing and in His way. I want Him to infuse into my mind what He wants me to tell you. I desire a knowledge and maturity beyond my own, and the capacity to share my heart. I am certain the Lord is going to see me through this latest step of faith.

As Providence would have it, when my problems began I was in the midst of teaching a Bible study on Philippians—the joy letter. I had even entitled the series, "Joy in the Journey." I'm confident now God was using that study to prepare me for the hard days I've experienced. Let's take a further look at those two words—*joy* and *journey.*

Joy

Do you detect little joy in the faces of the people you meet? Is joy evident in the lives of those in the traffic patterns of your life? There are so many who project the Christian life to be a monotonous, spiritless routine with little joy or excitement. One mental-health survey says only 20 percent of people are happy. What a sad commentary! Oliver Wendell Holmes said, "I might have been in the ministry if certain clergy that I knew had not looked and acted like undertakers." Do you know those who look and act like that? I do. Robert Louis Stevenson said, "I have been to church today and I am not depressed." This suggests something out of the ordinary. Maybe the missing ingredient that is keeping our churches from exploding in growth is the obviously missing note of joy in the lives of all of us.

We sing, "Joyful, joyful, we adore Thee," but if you look at people they are not really smiling. We need to start what someone has called an "epidemic of joy." William Barclay said, "There should be a sheer sparkle about the Christian life. Too often the Christian dresses like a mourner at a funeral." I have seen a few of those also.

One lady I met in Little Rock, Arkansas said, "A lot of people have Jesus in their heart, but they just haven't notified their faces yet." My husband says, "People walk around with their mouths looking like twenty minutes to four." They look like the night manager at the local mortuary! Observe those around you and see if you agree that joy is often missing.

Our faces are the windows of our hearts. Do you remember how the Pharisees disfigured their faces to be sure people knew they were fasting? They had lost their joy. The original purpose of fasting was self-denial and deeper communion with God. When that purpose was lost, communion with God was displayed as a grim, unhappy thing. Some people today still think it is. They think a long face is synonymous with Christianity. Not so—Satan is the one out to rob us of our joy.

Landrum regularly thanks one of our missionaries because he says she did more than any other person to convince me it was all right to marry a preacher. I had seen enough of these killjoys to conclude that no one in the world would want to be a minister's wife. At the time, I could not think of anything worse. Now I can't think of any greater joy. If I don't share anything at all with you except a positive attitude, this book will be worthwhile. For a long time I found little joy in service until I relaxed and found out serving the Lord was fun and fulfilling. I think we ought to work at being good witnesses and not let people think religion is a somber, depressing thing. The dominant note of Christianity is joy, which is nothing but the outward expression of the grace of God in our hearts. If you know Jesus, then you ought to possess real joy. Probably this missing ingredient is what attracted me to this subject.

Tim Hansel says in *Holy Sweat,* "If you have to move even ten inches from where you are right now to discover joy, I guarantee you will never know it."

Tony Campolo said, "Christians should create fun and excitement wherever they are placed." Do you radiate the love of Christ in the office where you work? Do you make a difference at the hospital where you nurse or in the classroom? If you don't, you should. Ps. 19:8 reminds us:

> The precepts of the Lord are right,
>   giving joy to the heart.
> The commands of the Lord are radiant,
>   giving light to the eyes (NIV®).

Our faces are an introduction of Jesus to others. Usually it is our faces more than our words that turn people off. Non-Christians will first be attracted to *you* before they are attracted to your message. A joyful spirit is contagious. If you had a choice, wouldn't you rather be around someone joyful than somebody negative, down, depressed, and critical?

Do you remember what the Scripture says about Stephen? "His

face was the face of an angel." I can't imagine a man being martyred who could still have a radiance on his countenance. Paul witnessed that, and I am convinced that experience, at least in part, is one of the things that brought Paul to Christ. I don't think he could ever get away from what he saw in the face of Stephen. That ought to convince us that our expressions are the most important things we wear, especially when they are joyful ones.

If I want to know something about joy, I am going to find a joyful person from whom to learn. We automatically think of the apostle Paul. A person who could sing praises in a jail at midnight must have the key. He knows something I want to know. In Philippians, Paul is sharing his secret of Christian joy. Prison is the last place from which to expect a letter of encouragement, but that is where Paul's letter originates. Paul's life was marked by pain, persecution, disappointments, adversity, physical beatings, and life-threatening events, but while in prison he wrote the Philippian letter, which is called the "joy book" of the New Testament. The unusual aspect of it is that there seemed to be no cause for rejoicing. Nineteen times in Philippians, Paul mentions joy, rejoicing, or gladness. It is a spiritual treat to count these. Phil. 3:1 says, "Finally, my brethren, rejoice in the Lord." In 4:4 he wrote, "Rejoice in the Lord always: and again I say, Rejoice." In Phil. 4:10, "But I rejoiced in the Lord greatly. . . ." What is the common phrase? *Rejoice in the Lord.* It is not just knowing the "plan of salvation" but the *man* of salvation.

Joy is one of the marks of a true believer. This is not a gushy emotion or a forced grin, but the security of knowing God's love. Joy and rejoicing come when we know Him and not in any other way. Most of us are looking for worldly solutions to spiritual problems. We think we are going to find joy in the substitutions of the world, but that is like putting water in a bucket with holes. Joy is found *only* in Jesus. It is not the absence of problems, or Paul would have had no joy, but the presence of the Lord. Paul was reduced to just having Jesus. Our circumstances don't determine our contentment but our faith and trust in God do. Paul refused to let circumstances dictate his joy. A Christian ought to be the happiest person alive.

Joy Defined

Before we go any farther, I want us to define the word joy. Joy is *not* a happy mask where you go around with a perpetual grin on your face. It is not a gushy emotion, but the result of the Lord living in us. When we were saved and invited Christ into our hearts, His promise was that He would come in and abide there. Joy is a deep emotional "wholeness" resulting from the secure knowledge that He is in us and with us.

Paul did not depend on place, position, possession, or even people for security and identity. Paul's confidence was not in another human being, or even in himself, but in the Lord. In Phil. 1:6 we read, "Being confident of this very thing, that He which hath begun a good work in you will perform it until the day of Jesus Christ." It is the trustworthiness of the Lord that gave Paul his confidence. If you take your eyes off Jesus, you are in *big* trouble. There are enough problems in life without adding stupidity to the list, and that is exactly what it is to think that human strength is sufficient for living these days. Christ was the source of Paul's strength, and He is the source for every Christian. His Spirit living in us is the *only* way we are going to be able to handle each day.

Believers have a point of beginning. What do we call it? Salvation, born again, conversion, redemption—all of these things describe the same experience. I like to call this "saving faith" as compared to "standing faith" and "serving faith," which I will discuss in later chapters. There is no abiding joy until Christ is the center of your life through saving faith. Saving faith moves you beyond words to the act of trusting your life to Jesus Christ. From the moment Paul was saved, he always looked back to his Damascus road experience as the beginning.

I did not have a Damascus road experience in the sense he had. I wasn't struck blind, or had scales on my eyes. We may not have had an experience identical to Paul's in manifestation, but we must have had one identical in transformation. We all have differing experiences, but if we are a child of God it began at some point in time.

I used to worry because I did not remember the day and hour I was saved. I began to doubt my conversion. My husband helped me here. He said, "Honey, do you remember when you were born?" I said, "No." He said, "But you know you were. It makes little difference if you remember the exact moment as long as you have the assurance of the reality that it has occurred." He said his daddy told him it wasn't how high you jumped when the Holy Spirit hit you, but how straight you walk when you come down!

Paul's encounter with Christ made all the difference. Just like the prodigal son, he "came to himself." My point of beginning is as much a *certainty* to me now as his was to him. Conversion is *not* automatic. You must have your own point of beginning. You can't make it on your husband's faith or his joy. You have got to ask that age-old question, "What must *I* do to be saved?" When we trust Jesus, He walks with us through our problems.

Do you have the *joy* of knowing that God has removed your sins and accepted you as His child? If not, you can. You have to decide to try God. When we accept Christ as real and as being with us always, we know joy in complete fullness. This is not just a higher level of life but ". . . ye rejoice with joy unspeakable and full of glory" (1 Pet. 1:8).

Up until 1990 I had lived a pretty calm, wonderfully blessed life. In fact, I entitled my first book *Don't Miss the Blessing* (Pelican Publishing Company). God has been so good to me in my journey through life—a wonderful home, a great husband, four loving children, and now eight precious grandchildren. God has been so good, and all this time He has "walked with me, and talked with me, and told me I was His own."

Don't misunderstand—my life has not been problem free. I have lost my mother, daddy, a sister, sister-in-law, and a brother recently. Nor has it been pain free—I have had normal illnesses until October 27, 1990, when the rug was pulled completely out from under me. I agree with Jill Briscoe, who said, "I found out I could cope with little spots of trouble quite well, but when lightning struck, I found it hard to keep singing."

When those trials come, if you are a Christian, if you are trusting Christ, then He is going to walk with you through these problems. He is going to be your strength. He is going to help, strengthen, and guide you. I have found that to be true in my journey. In the ups and downs of my pilgrimage, I've learned that we can acquire as much knowledge about God in the downs as in the ups of life. Yes, God is real for I have *experienced* Him, and I am so glad that I can count on His direction.

Distinguishing Joy from Happiness

I have always differentiated between joy and happiness. Happiness is dependent on circumstances or "happenings." In other words, if I get the new car I want, I am going to be happy. If I get that new sofa in my house, I am going to be happy. If my children behave today, I am going to be happy. Our happiness is dependent on happenings or circumstances.

Joy on the other hand is the outward expression of the inner experience of being loved. Do you ever stop to think how special it is that the Lord loves you? Do you bask in that love? I read the other day that children can make it if they know there is *one* person Who loves them. As Christians we can always know that one other Person loves us, and there is nothing comparable to that assurance. We may not always be able to count on our mate. Our children may disappoint us, and friends are sure to disappoint us, but we have one Person who loves us, and that is where joy originates. I like what someone said, that joy is ultimately rooted in an unshakable faith in God and springs from a deep conviction that God acts to save His people. I also like the title Warren W. Wiersbe gave to his commentary on Philippians: *Be Joyful, It Beats Being Happy.* The tendency to equate happiness and joy is rather common, but we soon learn that happiness is directly related to circumstances.

The dictionary defines joy as "an emotion evoked by well being, success, good fortune, delight, or by the prospect of possessing what one desires." I am sorry, Mr. Webster. That may define happiness, but it does *not* define joy. Life does not always give us success. Life does not always give us what we desire. In fact, if all difficulties were known at the outset of our journey, most of us would never begin. *Joy describes our connection with God.*

I imagine Paul could have thought of lots of other places he would rather have been than in jail. Yet he had joy. That excites me. I can guarantee you that problems will cause you to dig beneath the surface, but even in those difficult experiences you can know Jesus. The source of Paul's joy and ours is the inner experience of being loved and the assurance that God uses *everything* for our ultimate good . Isn't that what Rom. 8:28 says? "And we know that all things work together for good to them that love God, to them who are called according to His purpose." A more accurate rendering of the verse is, "God works all things together."

Years ago there was a professor named Caldwell. Concluding his lecture one day, he told his seminary students that he would lecture the next day on Rom. 8. He urged the students to study this chapter carefully, with special attention to verse 28. Then he spoke a final word affirming that special verse, with the reminder that regardless of what life brought, this verse would prove dependable.

That same day Dr. Caldwell and his wife met with a tragic car/train accident. She was killed instantly. He was crippled permanently. Months later, Dr. Caldwell returned to his students, who clearly remembered his last words. The room was hushed as he affirmed Rom. 8:28 as totally dependable. Though devastated in his grief, he was assured that one day he would discern God's good in this awesome tragedy.

I have come to the conclusion that faith is not delight in every terrible circumstance, but the settled assurance of the validity of that verse. "God works all things together for *good.*" Faith is confidence that all forces are ultimately under God's reign and power and He is taking care of the "working-together-for-good" process. God works behind the scenes in invisible ways. Faith is believing God is working even if you can't see Him working.

We don't know how He is working and we may not know for a long time after the fact. You have experienced things where you can look back and see how He worked. Whatever your particular set of circumstances, I'm confident you will be able to look back and see His hand in it. Joy is the settled assurance He is working all of these things together for good.

Notice that Professor Caldwell's emphasis is on God's good, *not* our temporary health, happiness, or prosperity. That perspective allows us to see our suffering and pain as bad in themselves, yet be reassured He is working in and through them to fulfill His purpose. As you get to those dark moments when circumstances are not ideal, when you miscarry or your baby dies, or your child disappoints you, keep Rom. 8:28 in mind. We can have the settled assurance of God's activity even in the midst of our sorrow and suffering.

Jill Briscoe said, "Christ cannot be contained within the tombs of our troubles, inside the sepulchers of our sorrows or behind the doors of our doubt." How true. My daily prayer became, "Help me, Lord, in this storm and when my faith is weak; help me to know that *You* are there even when I don't always feel Your presence." Joy is not the product of an hour's sermon or a week's seminar or a year's service. It grows in us as we yield to the Lord and serve others.

I want to tell you, even with my white hair, I still have trouble yielding and serving. It does not come easily. We must always put ourselves under His leadership and His will and let Him walk us through those problems.

Options Facing Us

Dr. John Sullivan said recently there are three possible attitudes to life. You can *regret* your life's status, you can *resign* yourself to your situation, or you can *rejoice* in God's love no matter what your condition. The ability to rejoice in any situation is a sign of spiritual maturity. Joy is a choice. Say no to negativism and choose to say yes to joy!

Habakkuk wrote in his prophecy, "Although the fig tree shall not blossom, neither shall fruit be on the vines; the labor of the olive shall fail, and the fields shall yield no meat; the flock shall be cut off from the fold, and there shall be no herd in the stalls: Yet I will rejoice in the Lord, I will joy in the God of my salvation" (Hab. 3:17-18). He described the direst of circumstances, but said, *"Yet I will rejoice in the Lord."*

It is so easy to focus on the downside of life rather than the positive side. We can *resent* adjustment; we can *react* with anger and resentment to our circumstances and those around us; or we can *respond* with joy and kindness. Which is it going to be with you? You have a choice. You can choose joy. When you meet those critical, negative people, you can be the one who changes the temperature. Some folks are determined to be miserable and make others miserable. Every one of us is as happy as we choose to be.

The thing that impresses me so about Paul was his ability to *choose* a joyful attitude even in the midst of *terrible* situations. How did it happen? I'll tell you how it happened. Because he depended *totally* on Jesus Christ. The verse even pagans can quote comes from his pen: "I can do all things through Christ Who strengthens me" (Phil. 4:13 NIV®).

Barbara M. Johnson wrote, "Pain is inevitable, but misery is optional." What were her qualifications for making this statement? She was the mother of four sons, one of whom was killed in Vietnam; another was killed in a car wreck by a drunk driver; a third graduated from high school with highest honors and promptly announced to the family that he was homosexual and disappeared, not to be heard of for years; and then her husband was in a car wreck and it was feared that he would remain a vegetable. Pain is inevitable, but misery is optional.

Women often set the thermostat in the homes. Hence the saying, "If Mama is having a bad day, the whole family is having a bad day. If Mama is having a good day, everybody else is having a good day." You can be the one who chooses joy as the dominant characteristic of your home. May the God of hope fill you with joy and peace as you trust Him.

Journey

Joy in the *journey*. There are many familiar Scriptures that mention journeys:

> Take nothing for your journey. (Luke 9:3)
> . . . took his journey into a far country . . . (Luke 15:13)
> . . . a Sabbath day's journey . . . (Acts 1:12)
> And as he journeyed, he came near Damascus. (Acts 9:3)
> . . . might have a prosperous journey by the will of God . . . (Rom. 1:10)
> Whensoever I take my journey into Spain, I will come to you. (Rom. 15:24)

The dictionary definition of the word is, "travel or passage from one place to another." I am suggesting we use the word to refer to our trip or passage through life. Each day is a journey. We can think of life as a series of moments, the sum of which is our journey. Yours really is a pilgrim's progress or "struggler's struggle." Never forget you are still in process. No believer is ever a finished product. You and I are not complete or will we ever be on earth.

We are not ever going to "arrive" at sinless perfection. We are just going to grow a little bit at a time.

Someone said, "Conversion of a soul takes a moment, but growth of a saint takes a lifetime." The last day you live I hope you will be growing. One of the saddest things I see is older people who drop out of Bible study. Now that they don't have to "set the example" for their children they become inactive. We say more to our children by what we do when we don't have to do it, than we did when it was required of us. God is bringing us along the road from infancy to adulthood, and we are carried forward through gradual development. If you are like me, about the time you think you may be maturing a little bit, you get thrown a curve like I was. I found out how little I knew about faith and trust. It is a lifelong process. We have to *be* before we can *become*.

"Instant" is a word that characterizes our time. Our instant, fast-food mentality affects our lives. Part of the frustration of our age is that the real needs and issues of life have no instant solution. Don't go to people who are grieving and suffering with an instant solution. We get laughed at sometimes because we quote a little Scripture and think that will handle everything. There are not any "Band-Aid" solutions. I did not find any in my wilderness experience. I wasn't healed instantly; my circumstances did not change overnight.

When tragedy strikes there are always seekers expecting instant solutions and cures. Salvation *is* a past act but will reach its full consummation only when Christ returns. Like the birth of a baby, the spiritual rebirth takes place at a particular time. It then continues as a lifelong process. If there was a shortcut to maturity *I* would have found it. The Christian life in Scripture is always presented in terms of movement, growth, and struggle. The building of Christian character takes *years*. It is a slow, steady pattern. The important thing is that we are heading in the right direction. When we repent of our sins, we turn from the old life to an entirely new direction. If you are headed in the right direction, I don't care how slowly you walk spiritually, it is okay. As long as you are taking little feeble steps of faith in the right direction, I'm confident our Father is pleased.

I will never forget when my daughter was dating the man she eventually married. He had grown up in our church in Texas. I knew his mother, daddy, and whole family. When it became obvious they were headed for the altar, I felt it was my duty to point out all of his bad qualifications while painting her daddy in perfection. She ended up using much more maturity than I did. She said, "Mama, I bet Daddy wasn't all that mature twenty-five years ago." She was exactly right. Why would I even expect a twenty-one year old to have the maturity of a fifty year old? Being saved does not mean that we instantly become like Jesus. It does mean that becoming like Jesus is our goal and we should never abandon it. Single-minded devotion to Him ought to be our passion.

My mother-in-law was my model, and one of the sweetest, godliest ladies I have ever known. I remember asking her how she was so patient, and kind. All she would ever say was, "Well, it is not easy." I was comparing myself to this fifty year old when I was just a young believer. We are so hard on ourselves.

Someone said, "It would be so easy if everyone was either saved or lost." We are saved, but in various stages of being saved. We are saved, but the process of sanctification goes on. That is why it is a sin to compare your life with another. It is a sin to compare new Christians with those who are twenty-five years old in the faith. When we do, we become critical of them. When you don't know the heart of someone or how hard he or she struggles, *don't judge*.

Self-Examination

What about *you*? Where are you in your faith? Are you growing? The sad commentary on many Christians is that from a spiritual standpoint their growth could be described as static, on hold, or nonexistent. Can you look back and see anything that lets you know some growth has taken place? I have so far to go, but I have come a long way. When I think of how I used to think and feel, I *know* the Lord has done a work in my life. Somewhere along the way my attitude changed and I know it wasn't me. He brought about the change from service being a chore to a blessing. Now there are not enough hours in a day for me to do what I want to do. I want to do *everything* at the church. I would take every job that's open. The hardest thing I have to do is say no. If we can look back and see progress, it encourages us and lets us know we are growing the right way. Then we just have to stay at it.

When you think of Paul, there was always a tension between where he was and where he wanted to be. In Rom. 7 he says there were things that he did that he didn't want to do. I want to have more faith than I do. I want to have a sweeter disposition than I have, but that is coming. The Lord is grinding off all the rough edges. It takes a lifetime, but He is getting me ready for eternity.

My problem is that I quarrel with the process. My husband has said through all of my recent experiences that my biggest problem was frustration. I have been *totally frustrated*. I want maturity and healing *now* instead of saying yes to the purifying process. All the Lord is doing is trying to mold me and make me, and I am kicking and screaming every step of the way. Corrie Ten Boom says, "We need to quit struggling and start snuggling."

They tell me a lifeguard who is trying to rescue a drowning person finds it almost impossible unless the person relaxes and cooperates—just floats. But what does a person who is drowning usually do? Thrash and grab and carry on, making it almost impossible to save him. That was a life-sized portrait of me. I find it so hard to relax and trust Christ.

Everything that has happened in my life has happened for a reason. It is part of my "becoming" process. If it were up to me I would erase all the painful parts. We don't like pain, but when we fight these experiences we rob ourselves of hard-earned wisdom. How could I ever develop faith and patience without trials to test me? Struggle seems to be His program sometimes. Like the butterfly, if we are released too soon the muscle-developing process of our wings will not have done its work.

I would never have known the depths of His love for me if I hadn't had this experience. I know He knows my personality and He knew it would take a *major* blowout for me because I am such a slow learner. It helps if we look at all the trials we face as possibilities to know God better. According to Watchman Nee, "We never learn anything new about God except through adversity." I prefer not to learn that way, but look back in your life at growth spurts. They probably came during problem times.

Through all this, I kept reprimanding myself for my lack of faith. Then I gained comfort these past months as I said to myself, "Even the incomparable apostle Paul had to learn." From his own pen he said, "I have learned to be content." Even Paul did not begin full grown in his faith. It, too, was a *journey*. Humility and dependence on Him are not bestowed, *they are learned*. I can't give them to you and you can't give them to your children. These are things everyone learns individually. Sorrow plows the fields for God's sowing and our harvest. It stretches our hearts and our usefulness for Him.

We let the Enemy press us beyond our measure of faith. If we can look at life's hard experiences as His training, then we can trust Him to take us through each schoolroom lesson as "we are able."

Joy is something we experience "in process"; it is not a destination. It is the result of the journey, and *not* something to seek. The point to remember is that every step we take in the journey we take in the Lord's own company.

My recent experience may have been a rod of correction to stop me dead in my tracks and to force me to take a hard look at where I had been and where I was going. Now I question my actions more than I used to and am careful always to ask His direction. When you can't do everything, you must be sure you are doing the right thing. Periodic self-examination is good and necessary to keep us in the center of God's will. Someone called it "the fine art of self-examination."

PRAYER

Lord, I am so grateful that joy runs deeper than the emotional rivers of happy or sad. Help me learn that no matter what befalls me, I can delight in my relationship with *You*. I can be joyful at all times and in all situations because I am Your child and You are my God!

Questions for Chapter 2

1) Write your own definition of "joy." Distinguish the difference between "joy" and "happiness."

2) What is your *attitude toward life?* Do you *regret* your life's status? Do you *resign* yourself to your situation? Do you *rejoice* in God's love no matter what your condition? Read Phil. 4:13 and rejoice with Paul in your own life situation.

3) Are you satisfied with your own journey through life? Where are you going and who is traveling with you?

CHAPTER 3

Journey through Dark Depression

DEPRESSION WAS AN UNFAMILIAR JOURNEY for me, to say the least. Of all the maladies I have ever imagined, this was at the bottom of the list. I guess that is why it came as such a shock when I began to encounter that "dark night of the soul." It is like a heavy cloud over and around you that you can't seem to escape—a bottomless black hole.

In my search for answers, this definition probably best summed up my feelings. "Depression comes when something of value is taken from us and a feeling of hopelessness and helplessness comes that leads to sadness." A form of paralysis sets in and brings one's life to a standstill.

Nancy Pannell, in her recent Broadman release, *Being a Minister's Wife and Being Yourself,* describes this condition:

> I know depression. It sneaked in the back door once and settled in before I recognized its presence. For a long while it wrapped around me like a heavy coat. It took on many forms. It was a weight so ponderous, even ordinary activities required great effort. It was physical pain, an aching in my chest. Most of all, it was deep sadness, an inexplicable sadness that triggered constant tears. No one, it seemed not even my husband, really understood how I felt. I wanted to escape the world.

One list of the sources of depression among women includes:

1) Low self-image.
2) Problems related to menstrual cycle.
3) Failure to share romantic love in marriage.
4) Sexual problems.
5) Poor time management and fatigue.
6) Money problems.

39

7) Problems among siblings.
8) Problems with in-laws.
9) Boredom and loneliness.
10) Problems related to aging.

I find it hard to believe that sickness and physical suffering were left off that list, unless it was assumed they went along with the aging process. It could be, however, these conditions are just now coming to the attention of mental-health practitioners because, until now, few people lived long enough to experience failing health. In 1960 the life expectancy was about forty-seven years of age. Today, it is seventy-five years. Because of that phenomenon, 15 to 25 percent of persons over the age of sixty-five will experience depression. It has been called the "common cold" of the emotions.

However, a new study of trends in major depression contends this is a worldwide phenomenon and is happening at younger and younger ages. A psychiatrist at Columbia University who helped compile the research says, "Since 1915 the risk has increased, nearly doubling for each successive generation. In general, the age when depression hits has fallen—from the late 20s in 1935 to between the ages of 15 and 20 after 1955." This study was compiled by research teams from the U.S. and eight other countries. According to their findings, in the U.S., one in four women and one in ten men will develop depression in their lifetime.

In my case, I'm confident the physical stress, fatigue, unanswered questions, and abnormal circumstances had taken their toll. Throughout my valley, Landrum always felt my biggest problem was total *frustration* resulting in discouragement. This statement is very true: "The measure of a man is the size of the thing that discourages." Here are some *D*s that can be a problem: 1) Despair, 2) Discouragement, 3) Disinterest, 4) Distress, 5) Despondency, 6) Disenchantment, 7) Depression.

Dr. George W. Truett called discouragement "disenchanted ego." Ouch! However, discouragement, and its full-grown fruit, depression, often plagued God's children.

I'm convinced the Lord has His own ways of getting our attention. As I began to write this chapter, my husband was away on business. I had planned for months to spend this week at my desk working on this manuscript. Now you have to understand when it comes to writing, I am a "draftee," *not* a volunteer! I feel that it is strictly a mandate from the Lord. There are a thousand things I would rather be doing. All week I had felt stress building up, dreading my commitment to "get at the task." If you are not a procrastinator, you probably cannot identify with my plight. I had spent two years reading and doing research for this book going through the ordeal I've described. I've had boxes of material labeled for each chapter ready for months for me to organize it and produce. As someone said, "My attention span is about the length of a commercial!"

Well, stress symptoms continued to plague me so my first thought was, "I'll just chuck the whole idea! Maybe the Lord doesn't want me to write." Quickly realizing the source of that thought, I began this chapter on discouragement and depression.

Now, back to the Lord's ways of getting my attention. The next morning I opened my Bible for my devotional reading, and the question faced me, "Why do we become discouraged?" David asked that question twice in Ps. 42:5,11. The answer is obvious—discouragement comes when we begin to *doubt God*, and question whether we are truly in God's hand and under His watchful care. Ouch again!

Every time I get uptight, frustrated, worried, irritated, or bogged down in self-pity, it is a lack of faith in God and the assurance of His Word. That morning He touched me anew with the assurance of His love, care, and direction—renewing my heart as spring renews the earth.

One of my doctors asked me at perhaps my lowest point, "Mrs. Leavell, are you afraid of dying?" I said, "Heavens no!" I am not afraid of dying, but I *am* afraid of getting out of the body! That is so often a long, arduous process, and I *am* afraid of a debilitating illness. No one of us would choose to live like that beyond our usefulness. We don't want to burden our children and lose all dignity at the mercy of others. When those terrifying thoughts cross our minds, we must go back to "what time I am afraid, *I will trust in Thee*" (Ps. 56:3). Sometimes I'm still afraid of dying, but I'm not afraid of death.

If we can just remember, God is at work even when He knocks out *all* the props. His arms will hold us when we are too weak to cling, and He gives us strength for our days! "Tho he fall, he shall not be utterly cast down, for the Lord upholdeth him with His hand" (Ps. 37:24). I *clung* to those words. Often we assume nothing is happening simply because we cannot see it happen. Like Thomas, we are "victims of the visible." But people who have the deeper wisdom believe God is working most when He is seen and felt the least.

Until my bout with depression, I never once realized how many of God's servants suffered from this malady. Saints in both the Old and New Testaments experienced it: Elijah, Jeremiah, Moses, Jonah, Paul, and even David.

Elijah went "a day's journey into the wilderness, and came and sat down under a juniper tree: and he requested for himself that he might die; and said, It is enough; now, O Lord, take away my life" (1 Kings 19:4).

Jeremiah said, "Cursed be the day wherein I was born" (Jer. 20:14).

Jonah prayed, "O Lord, take, I beseech thee, my life from me; for it is better for me to die than to live" (Jon. 4:3).

Paul, the incomparable apostle, mentioned trouble so severe "that we were pressed out of measure, above strength, insomuch that we despaired even of life" (2 Cor. 1:8).

The encouraging thing for us is the realization that God was not through with any of these servants. He went on to use each of them even though they encountered disillusionment, discouragement, and depression. They came through the trials believing and trusting God. In fact, it was from Paul's pen that we get that wonderful verse of assurance: "There hath no temptation taken you but such as is common to man: but God is faithful, Who will not suffer you to be tempted above that ye are able; but will with the temptation also make a way of escape, that ye may be able to bear it" (2 Cor. 10:13).

It always comforts me to read where David had some of my same complaints—though not about sickness. In Ps. 69 he says, "I am weary of my crying. . . . I am in trouble. . . . I am full of heaviness . . . hear me speedily" (verses 3, 17, 20).

I, too, became weary of crying. Tears seemed to be my constant companion. Landrum frequently had to act as my "interpreter" because I could not talk without resorting to tears. During those days I read many statements and Scriptures which carved themselves into my mind.

> "You have seen me tossing and turning through the night. You have collected all my tears and preserved them in your bottle! You have recorded everyone in your book" (Ps. 56:8 TLB). What a promise!
> "Tears wash the pain out of our hearts."
> "It's good to know that my tears for myself may be the prism needed to rediscover the rainbow that is me."
> "God keeps a costly school and many of its lessons are spelled out through tears." (If that is true, I should have learned a bunch!)

John was old when he wrote the Revelation and the journey had taken its toll, yet he assures us: "And God shall wipe away all tears from their eyes; and there shall be no more death, neither sorrow, nor crying, neither shall there be any more pain: for the former things are passed away" (Rev. 21:4).

Tears are humanity's lowest common denominator. I am so glad God knows and understands my tears. I am an "easy crier," which proved to be a healthy response to my situation. The Scripture says, "When Jesus therefore saw her [Mary] weeping, and the Jews also weeping which came to her, He groaned in the Spirit, and was troubled" (John 11:33).

I often encountered the opposite effect. One of my doctors, who was completely lacking in a "bedside manner," asked me at one point, "Mrs. Leavell, are you always this emotional?" Can you imagine? And he was a married man—do you suppose he had never seen a woman cry? I absolutely wanted to *kill* him and tell the Lord he died!

It was to that same doctor that I later wrote this letter:

March 24, 1990

Dear _____,

I started to call you, but maybe I can express myself better this way since I am so prone to tears. Let me try to explain where I am coming from, and why I have been concerned, fearful, apprehensive, or whatever you want to call it.

From my initial problem on October 27th with numbness in Baton Rouge, I have been passed around to a total of seven doctors. In four months I have had just about every test known to man, and many of them more than once. I've had two MRIs, worn the heart monitor twice, had an angiogram, and have had four EEGs—coming up on five [later seven!]. I appreciate the effort that has been put forth in my behalf, but what has been lacking is any explanation of what seems to be going on.

The mitral valve prolapse I can live with, but the EEGs worry me. My questions are:

1) Is there any change in the four—worse or better? If there is change then it probably isn't congenital but nobody has told me. You did say there was no change in the last two.

2) Do the irregularities go away with time or are they permanent?

3) Do you think a TIA (transient ischemic attack) caused them?

4) What else could the irregularities be an indication of? I'm convinced the unknown is worse than the known.

5) Are both sides of the brain affected or is it just one side?

6) Is the numbness I am experiencing in my hands at night in any way related?

7) Do you see many situations like mine?

8) How serious is my problem?

From a patient's viewpoint, a sympathetic discussion of the situation would be helpful. The idea seems to be "you are worrying unnecessarily," but that is what any woman will do without some explanation.

[Another doctor] has been especially helpful in trying to pull all of this together, but of course, he refuses to speak as an authority in your area of expertise.

I would appreciate a call or I'll be glad to come in if you think it necessary. I'll be leaving town Thursday afternoon for ten days so hope to talk to you before then.

Thank you for your attention to my concerns.

Sincerely,
Jo Ann Leavell

This same doctor is the one who said amidst my tears, "Mrs. Leavell, I think you need to see a psychiatrist." At that point, if somebody had told me I needed to see a veterinarian, I probably would have done it!

I chose a woman who came highly recommended, and my rationale was, she had probably seen tears before and maybe even experienced them—at least monthly! Kidding aside, I just felt I could talk more openly about my weird feelings to a woman. I'm convinced the Lord led me to that decision because she became like a friend and was a part of my climb out of the pit.

Doctor-Patient Relationships

After my experiences, I have come to believe it is just as important to shop carefully for a doctor as it is for any other major decision. My friend Grace Chavis says, "We women will shop for hours for just the right groceries or just the right clothing store, but we will not shop around for the right doctor."

Somehow, me included, we are intimidated by the medical profession. Chavis points out, "Doctors are not gods—they are highly trained human beings. Their training and their reputation are important, but so are their abilities to listen to you and to understand your feelings."

In my defense, I would have changed doctors had I not felt I would be put through that same testing process *again*. Knowing what I know now about the importance of the doctor-patient relationship, I believe I would have taken the risk.

I had to pray hard about my attitude toward that doctor. It would have been so easy to *react* rather than *act*. We are seldom shown in advance God's intention in a particular trial, nor the long-term effect our actions may have on others. My prayer, through it all, was that I would be the right kind of witness.

The good news is that my primary-care physician is the most loving, caring man I have ever encountered. I would have gone completely *under* without his interest and skill.

The Reality of Fear

However, my fears and tears continued without end. Everything I had nailed down had come loose. Life was no longer in working order. I kept reminding myself that "fear intrudes on every life." It is "the agitated state of mind that cripples us from looking any further than the hardship itself." In subjective depression, we see our problems magnified and distorted. Fear is holding mental pictures of the worst things that could possibly happen. Fear roams the hallways of our minds and we get stuck in a cycle. It is the most destructive force in our personalities.

JOURNAL ENTRY

> Why, oh why? I guess I'm uptight about having another EEG today. You already know what the results are going to be, and I've got to trust Your perfect will.
>
> My reading this morning was from Job—"Though I say, I will forget my complaint, I will leave off my sad countenance and be cheerful, I am afraid of all my pains" (Job 9:27 NAS). I feel exactly the same way and I am afraid—I wish I wasn't, but I am. Help me.

I *know* what fear is—believe me! The last engagement I filled before canceling my engagements was a ladies' retreat for First Baptist Church, San Antonio. We were to drive out of San Antonio to a motel in Kerrville, Texas for the Friday and Saturday get-togethers where, incidentally, we had relatives living.

The closer the weekend got, the more disturbed I became. When I thought of flying alone, staying alone, and traveling alone I absolutely wanted to run. *Panic* best described my feelings.

I did something I had never done before (or since), but I literally *begged* Landrum to go with me. We would be back before he had to leave for his Sunday engagement. I gave him every reason I could think of—"you can study, rest, relax . . ."—except the main one: I was afraid to go alone! Of course, he sensed my predicament and agreed to go. (Thank the Lord for frequent-flyer points!)

We made the trip, and since my meeting involved supper, he called his cousins to meet him for the night meal. So far so good—*until* he announced to me they were not eating at the motel but were going into town. This thought had never entered my mind, and again, *sheer panic.* I didn't want him that far away.

Until you have felt as I felt, you can never know how one feels in such a situation. I literally thought "dying" was a live possibility, and

I surely didn't want to die among strangers! It sounds ludicrous now, but believe me, at the time it was a serious matter.

Again, my husband sensed my fear, remained at the motel, and I calmed down enough to get through my responsibilities that night. As an aside, let me tell you that I got some of the most positive evaluations I have ever received, which bears out the truth of 2 Cor. 12:9—"My power shows up best in *weak* people" (TLB). It also bears out the truth that "the power for ministry does not come from *my* strength." Thank goodness!

You say, "Jo Ann, where was your faith in God?" My faith was there—I knew where I would spend eternity—but as the little boy said, "I needed somebody with skin on!" I thank the Lord for my loving, sensitive husband.

Yes, fear is real, even among Christians, and the answer for unreasonable fear is reasonable trust. In times of raw panic, the Lord will provide His care. Walk up to the fear, admit the possibility of what you fear most, look it full in the face, but never forget we don't have to face challenges or overcome difficulties alone. Divine help *is* available.

JOURNAL ENTRY

I continue thinking and reading about my "nothingness." Help me to realize, however, that is one of the conditions for receiving Your power. We are *not* to depend on our own faith, but on *Your* faithfulness. I don't have to apologize for my weakness—I keep trying to depend on my faith and it is weak at times. I only need faith to trust You and know You love me because of Who You are, not because of what I am.

How to Respond to Fear

What do you do when fear arises? Entertain it, encourage it, or enjoy it? Complain like a child or take charge of it like an adult? At this point there was little, if any, "take charge" left in me. However, even at my worst, I knew I had a choice, and these were my three options. I could:

1) *Entertain my fears,* which is an unhealthy focus on self. I read, "Fear often grows out of an unhealthy focus on self: self-love, self-

concern, self-centeredness, self-protection." That is not a very pretty picture, is it? And *nothing* robs one's strength and vitality like self-absorption. When our eyes are that focused on self, there is *no way* they can be focused on God.

Tribulation is sometimes necessary for the decentralization of self. There are many lessons learned *only* in the school of suffering. Our job is to focus on Him—not the problems. "Put your *focus on living in Him* . . . and fruit is inevitable" (John 15:1-17). "My joy might remain in you and . . . your joy might be full" (verse 11).

JOURNAL ENTRY

This morning I woke up feeling tense and worried. That's Satan again—he loves to push us to worry and despair—to distress and depress us. I don't want to let go—give him a victory—out of sheer weakness. Help me to understand these attacks from him and how to resist them.

My pastor preached recently on brokenness—God is breaking our will but *not* crushing our spirit. He is gentle. Gen. 32 is a pattern we *all* eventually follow. I'm there!

Aloneness—Gen. 32:24a—This is *my* battle. All the props are gone.

Struggle—verse 24b—God lets us struggle that we may yield to Him and His will.

Brokenness—verse 25—God can only use us fully if we are broken.

Endurance—verse 26—God will not turn away those who hold on. What a comfort!

Blessing—verse 28—God uses and changes broken people to bless the world. I'm so glad.

Satan's goal is to create joyless souls. When he finds a weak spot in our faith, he is pleased. He doesn't want us to make the journey to the mountain, but to settle for living in the valley. I have a precious friend who calls often, and encourages me with Scripture and her unusual wisdom. She constantly reminds me that when Satan can upset me, he has the victory. He will manipulate me with the mysterious and taunt me with the unknown—fear of death, failure, God, tomorrow. Satan's target is our mind. He can cause a negative attitude quickly to overshadow God's beautiful promises.

Face those fears, and give them permission to exist. The more fervently we believe we shouldn't be having our feelings, the more pronounced those feelings seem to be. Move forward against your fears with God's help, and those fears can become the catalyst for an overcoming faith. "Once you've looked back, you are ready to move forward." When I get wrapped up in my own worries, I sometimes forget Who has never failed to ease them in the past! Never forget: "It is His past provision that gives us the greatest hope for the future."

Another option is to:

2) *Encourage my fears.* This is an excerpt from my journal.

> I read today about fear and it was just for me. I've been so afraid lately—my feelings, my health, stress, the future, and everything else. My problem is *dwelling* on the wrong things. Help me not to *"feed my fears."*

My sister said to me one day, "I never thought I would be depressed." Well believe me, I didn't either! It just proves that we never know what challenges we are going to face. Somehow we think we are *beyond* problems, but problems give us the opportunity to learn something. Frequently, if we don't learn completely the first time, the next whack will be a little harder.

My "resoluteness" (bullheadedness) must have come from my father. He, too, was a slow learner. I remember well the day he came in from the golf course, rang the doorbell, and when I went to the door he was lying down on the floor unable to make the stairs (we lived on the second floor). He was having chest pains, and in spite of warnings from his doctor, *he* concluded it was just a case of slight indigestion. That is, until the second whack came with a full-fledged attack, and he became a believer!

I wrote this as I looked out over the majestic mountains in North Carolina. While Landrum had been engaged in meetings that week, I had been able to take advantage of the local scenery and culture. The mountains were so beautiful and just another reminder of God's goodness and creative power.

One day I toured the John C. Campbell folk school. This is a school endowed by a man seeking to keep alive mountain lore, where they teach crafts native to this part of North Carolina. I saw people engaged in wood carving, pottery making, quilting, basket weaving, but of special interest to me was the blacksmith shop.

It was a *hot* July afternoon, and I'm still wondering how those would-be craftsmen stood the heat from the fires used to mold the iron. The class was being taught to take a long piece of wrought iron and to give each end a scroll-like effect through repeated heatings. As I watched the iron being put in and out of the fire as it was twisted and hammered, it gave new meaning to the phrase "mold me and make me." It reminded me anew that the certainties of our faith are often fashioned like steel in the white-hot fires of adversity.

Every time the iron became cold and hard, it went back in the fire. I came away from that tour praying, "Lord, help me stay warm and pliable so I won't have to go back in the fire." We get many opportunities to learn the lessons we need to learn. I'm trying *hard* to listen carefully to the Lord and not require further discipline.

I still remember how, when I was disobedient, my daddy would make me go out and cut a switch for him to administer punishment. If I cut one that was too small, he would just send me right back. I can still remember how that switch would sting my legs, and if I ever ran from him the *worst* sting was at the end of the switch. Could it be with our loving Heavenly Father that the closer to Him we are the less the whipping hurts?

One doctor gave me food for thought when he said, "Mrs. Leavell, the tendency to depression may have always been there and you were too busy to notice." My "work" addiction had functioned as a giant tranquilizer.

As I look back, there have been other times when my emotions were in control and stress was a factor. The year I finished college was one of those. I was studying for finals, planning a wedding, and my mother had been experiencing health problems my entire senior year. Most of us pay little attention to multiple stress points until they have physical implications. My hair began to come out— whole hands full! Now, *that* will get your attention! I went to the doctor and was told stress was the culprit.

Another time involved extreme *jealousy* resulting from the low self-esteem I shared in *Don't Miss the Blessing*. The connection between diminished self-esteem and depression has long been known. Anyone whose self-esteem has been eroded is more prone to depression, which probably explains why more women than men become depressed. For a variety of reasons, women clearly tend to experience lower self-esteem than men.

Landrum was scheduled to do a revival in Birmingham, Alabama when he had a call from an old girl friend. She lived in that area and had seen the publicity in the paper. She assured him she would be at the services, and was looking forward to seeing him. I was *livid!*

With four children still at home, I rarely went with him in those days. However, I moved heaven and earth, arranged for the children, and planned to accompany him to Birmingham. During the intervening weeks, I became angry, depressed, lost weight, and was in a "state" by the time the week arrived.

I can honestly say, however, that my decision to go with him was one of the *best* decisions I have ever made—bar none! From the moment I saw her, *all* fear, jealousy, hurt, and anger left me. Had I not gone and faced the situation head on, I might have "fed my fears" until they became a real problem in our marriage. Something can be said for facing our fears head on to relieve stressful situations even though it is not pleasant.

My attitude during those brief experiences was "this too shall pass." The only difference between those and my "recent" journey is that this problem appears to have come to stay!

I'll have to confess, however, that that is an answer to prayer. My walk with the Lord during those dark days was so sweet, I asked Him to "just keep me weak enough to constantly depend on *You.*" I guess the moral of that story is, be *very* careful how you pray, it just may be answered! Now, every time the telltale signs of stress appear, I have to back off and say, "Okay, Lord, I'm listening!"

It is so easy constantly to feed and encourage our fears as we play the tapes in our head over and over. These negative messages we repeatedly give ourselves are the root of depression. I can identify with David as he prayed, "The troubles of my heart are enlarged: O bring thou me out of my distresses" (Ps. 25:17). It is as though we think we can *prevent* the worst by anticipating it! Worry does not cure anything—it just adds another problem. Worry is concern without prayer. This anxious spirit means we are not trusting God.

I could also:

3) *Enjoy my fears.* When we face our fears and let ourselves know

our connection to the power that is in us and beyond us we learn courage. Nothing will put an end to all murmuring and rebelling thoughts except seeing God in *everything.* "It is the Lord: let Him do what seemeth good" (1 Sam. 3:18). The good news is, of all people in America who suffer deep depression, more than 95 percent fully recover.

I've got to remember that "at the very heart and foundation of all God's dealing with us, however dark and mysterious it may be, we must dare to believe in and assert the infinite, unmerited and unchanging love of God." *Love* permits *pain,* but remember "the Lord is nigh unto them that are of a broken heart; and saveth such as be of a contrite spirit" (Ps. 34:18).

JOURNAL ENTRY

I'm reading in John 15-16 and over and over it says, "I am loved and chosen" and "Ask anything and I will do it." I don't know all that refers to, but I'm asking for healing and an end to my depression. But if I never get any better, I'm grateful for the healing I've already received. At least I can function and I couldn't even do that for awhile. Thank You for what You've done and are going to do.

Last Christmas my sister-in-law gave me a daily calendar for women who do too much! I'm not sure I should have thanked her for it because each morning as I tear off those pages, I see myself and the picture is not very flattering.

What about you? Are you overextending your physical limits? Is busyness a cover-up for your failure to deal with deeper matters? Are you failing to work through anger in any of your relationships? It is important to express emotions appropriately and not harbor bitterness, which leads to depression. Some have suggested "depression is simply anger turned inward."

I felt that anger was one part of the "grief process" I had avoided until I read that statement. Perhaps I have been angry over my wings being clipped and didn't realize it. Maybe the second whack for me was my depression, and believe me, to quote one fellow sufferer, "There ain't nothin' like a whuppin' from the Lord."

Confront Fear with Love

Trials, conflicts, battles, and testings along the way are not to be counted as misfortunes, but rather as a part of necessary discipline. I agree with the woman who said she was learning to welcome pain, and not to dodge it. It is true that pain has a refining work to do in us, if we welcome it. Through pain we can learn what is temporal and superficial and what is abiding and deep. Pain has a way of doing its work in us if we let it.

I'm trying not to remain in the "shadows" of distrust, but to walk by faith, *not feeling.* "Feelings" are emotions, *not* fact—forgive me for "groveling on the low ground," as someone put it, "of emotion and feeling." Remember, it is *fighting* our feelings that causes our suffering, not the feelings themselves. The basic discipline is to learn to believe against feelings. Feelings most often can be a result of believing but seldom the basis for believing.

I asked the Lord to help me maintain my joy in the midst of my circumstances, a "holy composure," as someone described it. I'm continually reminded that: "The best things of life come out of wounding! Human nature seems to need suffering to fit it for being a blessing to the world."

Fear remains today as a great hindrance to a full and abundant life. We need to fear some things such as loaded guns, hateful attitudes, and prejudice. These are legitimate areas of concern. But to face other concerns such as health problems and unemployment requires a special strength that comes *only* through Jesus Christ. We're built to overcome all fear. Being afraid is not a sin, but we must embrace the threatening disaster and move ahead in obedience. Confront fear with love—not "what will happen to me?" but "what can I do for others?" Our choice is to change our thinking outwardly—through actions. God can always use our adversity for His glory. You will never grow more than your last barrier.

An older minister advised a group of young pastors: "If you will *always preach to broken hearts,* you will be an up-to-date preacher." One thing binds us all together: we are sufferers. I found that those who walk through the valley of the shadow of death do not walk alone. God becomes a cosufferer through the gift and death of His own beloved Son. The Psalmist reminded us in the Twenty-third Psalm that we would *not* be left in the valley. So I have hope. The problems that I feel are unique to me have existed in some form in other eras. Jesus knows about them and how they can be solved. Even more important, He cares for us and will not leave us without strength to cope. One thing we *know:* "For God hath *not* given us the spirit of fear; but of power, and of love, and of a sound mind" (2 Tim. 1:7).

The Scriptures are full of verses promising joy after pain. Paul said to Timothy in 2 Tim. 1:4, "Recalling your tears, I long to see you, so that I may be filled with *joy*" (NIV®). Probably Timothy wept the last time he and Paul had parted, and Paul recalled that tearful parting. However, what that verse says to me is soothing tears and helping others result in *joy.*

The message of the Resurrection was first given to a group of women. "So the women hurried away from the tomb, *afraid yet filled with joy*" (Matt. 28:8 NIV®). They were instructed to begin a missionary ministry to "go quickly and tell His disciples" (verse 7). The reason for the urgency was the disciples were in a well of deep depression. They were discouraged and needed to hear the truth. Jesus later appeared to the twelve to help them overcome their lack of faith.

Elijah prayed to die, yet the Lord reassured him and commissioned him for further work. David prayed in Ps. 40, "O Lord, make haste to help me," and he said, ". . . the Lord heard, brought him out of the pit, stabilized him, and put a new song in his heart that many shall see and trust the Lord" (verses 2-3). Through my tears I claimed the promise, "Weeping may endure for a night, but *joy* cometh in the morning" (Ps. 30:5). *And it did!*

PRAYER

Lord, thank You that You care for me and that not even the salty tears of discouragement and depression can wash away Your love. Help me to release my grip on all those cares that trouble me and not sweat the small stuff. Protect me from going beyond the limit where burnout brings disillusionment, discouragement, and depression. Help me take time—make time—for rest, relaxation, and renewal.

Questions for Chapter 3

1) Have you ever experienced depression, a sense of hopelessness and helplessness? How has God helped you to cope with it?

2) What fears obsess you? How has your trust in God helped you respond to fear?

3) Read 2 Tim. 1:7 and describe how God replaces fear.

CHAPTER 4

Slowing Down for the Journey

PROBABLY THE AREA MOST AFFECTED by the experiences I've shared is my expenditure of time. I've taught many a class on time management even as I have on the importance of our up-to-date walk (journey) with the Lord. Looking at these from a new perspective, I wouldn't change a thing I've said except to emphasize *both* with new conviction. Honey, you simply *must* prepare for bad days in good days—and that will *not* happen without proper goals and priorities.

I have had time to think in a way I have never had before. When doctors slow you down, all you can do is think. So I am going to share with you some of the things I have been thinking about the last several months. A lot of it has to do with my stewardship of time.

Situation

Let's look first at the *situation*. We live with the "tyranny of the clock." It is always there before us. I walked into my motel room recently while attending a conference, and the first thing I saw was this *big* digital clock. It was just another reminder of the fact that we live by a watch. The clock plus the pace today equals a scarcity of time. We all experience it. There really is a universal fatigue that goes along with the pace we keep.

Mary Crowley, who for years until her death ran "Home Interiors" (you have probably been to a "Home Interiors" party), said, "Fatigue is the greatest enemy of women." Men have wives. We don't have anyone to help us in the rat race. I love this paraphrase of Ps. 23.

The clock is my dictator, I shall not rest.

It makes me lie down only when exhausted.
It leads me to deep depression.
It hounds my soul.
It leads me in circles of frenzy for activity sake.
Even though I run frantically from task to task,
I will never get it all done,
For my "ideal" is with me.
Deadlines and my need for approval they drive me.
They demand performance from me,
Beyond the limits of my schedule.
They anoint my head with migraines.
My in-basket overflows.
Surely fatigue and time pressures shall follow me all the days of
    my life,
And I will dwell in the bonds of frustration forever.

Now, isn't that the way we feel? We get caught up in this whirlwind. There seems to be a compulsive drive within us that will not rest. Men and women set out at a tremendous speed to go nowhere.

I remember a story about an airline pilot who came on the loudspeaker and said, "I've got good news and bad news. The good news is we are making great time. The bad news is we don't know where we are." I look around at people and see harried looks, and wonder if they have any idea where they are going. What about you? Do you have a clue what life is all about, and where you are going at this breakneck speed? What is the reason behind this harried existence? We are speeding through life pursued, it seems, by the demon "hurry."

When she was four, my little granddaughter taught me a great lesson. Most of my family is like me, wired pretty tightly. Gentry is more like her mother who operates at a little slower pace. When I held Gentry's hand and walked across campus, she could not be hurried. If you tried, she just let go of your hand. It occurred to me one day, that four year old is smarter than her grandmother. I let people hurry me, but she *would not*. Her daddy got frustrated with her on one occasion. I said, "Oh, let her alone. She will live a lot longer than we will."

Someone said, "Our modern society is sucked as dry as a lemon, and almost as sour." We are sour in the midst of our hurry, and really not very pleasant to live with. Life *is* hectic. Most of us are carried along in the wake of change moving so rapidly that we can't keep up. I'm told the rate of change in a person's life is generally predictive of future health. We are doing something to ourselves when we keep up this pace day in and day out. We somehow forget that this computerized society in which we live is taking its toll on us, and on our personal needs.

In our Western society those hardest hit by this are middle-class, white-collar workers—professional people, working women with children, and even clergy. The reality is that there *is* an information overload, and time "to think" is the rarest of commodities. There is no time anymore to think, rest, or pause from the frenzy to let your soul catch up with your body. Someone said, *"If the devil can't make you bad, he will make you busy."* Is that scary or what? We pride ourselves on not being bad. The same thing may be accomplished with everything being done in haste.

Most of us are so tomorrow-oriented we do not enjoy the present moment. I am as guilty as you are. One of the ways we evidence this is at mealtime. We don't sit down and have meals together anymore. We get food on the run. I talked to a career woman recently. She said for years she had eaten fast food or not eaten at all because of her busy life. That is not good. Most of us either eat the wrong food or eat the right food in the wrong way, which is in a hurry. You can imagine what that does to your digestive tract. We need to bring our families back to the table for meals and conversation.

I was on a panel in New Orleans recently with a group of ministers' wives. There were four of us from different denominations and different walks of life. One of the ladies said in a whiny voice, "My husband is gone 95 percent of the time. He is never home and I just have to be Mother and Daddy." She went on and on until I wanted to *die.* My urge was to get in her face and say, "If he is gone 95 percent of the time, that's *your* fault." I don't care where he is pastor, he does not have to be gone all the time. At some point we have got to assume control of our own lives. Don't go through life blaming everyone else. You *do* have time. You *can* take charge of your life and pick out the activities you are going to be involved in.

You *can* sit down for meals if that is a priority with you. We *can* set our own agendas.

Another way the "tyranny of the clock" shows up is in our exercise. Listen to this: "Intensive kinds of exercise are the most popular." Why? You can do them in a hurry. This is that pressure again. Even our exercise is at a fast pace.

Sleep is affected. My middle son is in a pressure-cooker business—a church bond business. He is the only one in the business who travels and hustles those bond issues, which are their bread and butter. He fights deadlines all the time. He had never been a jogger until recently. We had tried to get him to exercise, but there was no interest.

He played college basketball on scholarship. To be sure you stayed in shape during the summer, a ten-mile run was required in the fall. He *hated* it. I think he promised the Lord if he ever got out of school he would never jog again. All of a sudden, my daughter-in-law said, "Mom, Roland is jogging *every* night." I registered my surprise. She said, "You know what did it? When he got in the bed late one night and was so wired he could not sleep." I guess he decided he had to get some relief from tension and stress.

Today's hectic life-styles guarantee that stress-related insomnia and daytime sleepiness won't soon vanish. In our high-tech age, there are just too many reasons to stay awake. Someone said, "We have twenty-four-hour supermarkets, all-night television, and people who are forced to work late shifts and sleep out of sync with their body's clock. One hundred years ago, when the sun went down, people went to bed." That's not a bad idea!

We disregard our biological rhythms. Do you know you have a weekly rhythm? Most women are aware of a monthly rhythm, but we even have an annual rhythm. When we disregard this, we are asking for trouble. I'm told we do our best work in three-hour units with a break every one and a half hours. When we disregard these things our health is affected. Shift workers are really affected by these interruptions of rhythms and are more vulnerable to physical and marital breakdowns as a result. I was especially interested in this because my oldest son pastored for six years in an area composed mainly of shift workers.

Jet travelers also are familiar with changes in the biological rhythms. One of our professors had been on sabbatical. He was in

Europe, and immediately after returning went to Hawaii. I saw him soon after and asked, "How is it going?" He said, "I am doing okay, but my body is not even speaking to me!" Have you ever felt like your body wasn't speaking to you? This is what happens when we don't pay attention to our biological rhythms. We become incapable of relaxing and sleeping properly.

I sat in a stress seminar at Ridgecrest Baptist Assembly one summer. The one thing I remember the speaker saying was, "We must learn to relax without going to sleep." If I relax I am *gone,* so I have not mastered that yet.

I'm told it takes an hour to unwind before you genuinely relax. When I read that statement to my husband he said, "Honey, that is what I'm doing in my easy chair in the afternoon!" Often when our children were small I used to resent his ability to relax so quickly. I told him the only way his family was going to remember him was laid out in his recliner with his mouth open!

At the seminary, he insists employees take their *whole* vacation at one time. You say, that is a dirty trick. No, I think it is because of this very fact. If you take one day here, and three days there, you are not gone long enough to relax. If you have a two-week vacation, it takes you a week of it to get in the position to enjoy the rest. Then you come back to your job refreshed.

All too frequently, we read only for profit, play only for exercise, and just see how many miles we can clock up. I am as guilty as I can be. I imagine some of you are, too. Many of us are well off financially, but we are paupers when it comes to time. Do I need to remind you that "freedom from greed is freedom from time"?

One of the reasons we don't have time is because many are moonlighting to make more money. However, women are often the ones who push their husbands into taking on another job. Who says that you can't live on less? Who says that you can't live in a smaller house if necessary? You see, happiness has a way of fleeing those who try to buy it! I am afraid we are in a society caught up in this desire to have just a few more things.

Think about this statement: "A scale of living and luxury ill-proportioned to the income, will soon tire the one who pays the bills." It's sad, sad, sad. We believe in Jesus, but we draw our meaning from positions, possessions, and people. When we are so wedded to the world, we lose sight of the spiritual and lose our *joy.* The bottom line is that there is more to life than the bottom line. Don't you want more than a nice house, two cars, and a two-week vacation every year?

It has been said that the three *P*s of yuppiedom are prosperity, prestige, and power. Most of us want all the world has to offer and heaven, too. You can't tell the difference between a Christian and a non-Christian by the things they want. I'm guilty. I want these same things. I enjoy the good life, but I don't want it at the expense of my home, my health, or my witness to others.

The situation is not very pretty, is it? We must go back to the passage in Rom. 12:2 that says, "Don't let the world around you squeeze you into its own mold, but let God remold your minds from within" (Phillips). We are being squeezed into the mold of the world, and there is a "barrenness of busyness." What is the cure? What is the way out of this dilemma? There are several.

Solutions

The first is what the hippies did back in the sixties. They had this quest for a "fuller experience" and rejected everything of a materialistic nature. They sought the spontaneous, and they did it through alcohol, music, drugs—"trips" from reality. Their motive was good, but their method was faulty. This gave only temporary relief from the problem. Needless to say, a temporary escape is *not* a permanent solution. We must deal with the problem, not evade it. So the hippies had no answer for us.

Others have chosen alcohol. Studies indicate alcoholics often are just reacting to their regulation and speed at work. Drinking speeds up their leisure. The "tyranny of the clock" is an ever-present problem. I hope I don't need to tell you alcohol is not the answer.

Others have a complete nervous breakdown. "Physical and nervous breakdown is for many people the only way out of the impasse." Paradoxically, it is a healthy response to the problem because it springs from a deep-seated cry that "enough is enough." Granted, it is an extreme solution and not one I would recommend. However, those whom you know in this condition need compassion, *not* criticism.

Occasionally premature death occurs. We work ourselves into an early grave on this materialistic merry-go-round. A manifestation of our self-hate is the way we drive ourselves beyond our energy.

Solitude

I think the better *solution* is an alternative life-style. I have come to see this as the only permanent solution to an ever-increasing problem. Many people see our situation as a *fact of life* rather than a condition to be changed. This is not so. We must learn to *act,* not just *react,* and take control of our lives. It is so tempting to place blame: "they" pushed me into this or "she" made me assume this role. One of the signs of maturity is taking responsibility for our own actions.

Mark 6:31 says, "Come ye yourselves apart into a desert place, and rest a while: for there were many coming and going, and they had no leisure so much as to eat." Ps. 1:2 reads, "But his delight is in the law of the Lord: and in his law doth he meditate day and night." Zech. 2:13 says, "Be silent, O all flesh, before the Lord: for He is raised up out of His holy habitation." Hab. 2:20: "But the Lord is in His holy temple: let all the earth keep silence before Him." Finally, Job 4:16 says, "There was silence, and I heard a still voice." What was the key idea in those passages? *Silence.* The solution is to be silent, to pray, and to wait for God.

I'm told you teach best what you have the hardest time learning. I can teach with authority on this subject because I have had the hardest time learning it. It is not my nature to be quiet. It is *hard* for me to wait for the Lord, but a fast-paced life *can* become an opiate. I have thrived on activity and pressure, flying along on the adrenaline of frenzy. That has been my life-style. I don't know how many of you can relate to this. Some people fight pressure and a harried existence, but I am addicted to it! I like having more things out there than I can possibly accomplish. It becomes a challenge.

We have eight grandchildren. I like nothing better than to get them all together, and the wilder it gets the better I like it. My husband, on the other hand, is liking chaos less and less. He wants them one at a time or not at all.

If I were guessing, I could divide those reading this into two groups: those who need to slow down, and those who need to speed up! There are some of you doing absolutely nothing. *Do something.* Some stress is good. It has been proven that we work better under stress, but *not* to the breaking point. The solution for those like myself is to *slow down.* It sounds absurd but we can make better time by slowing down. Where do you fit in?

Meditation is the crucial answer to our problem. Not until our engines cut off do we face the sobering realities that inactivity and silence bring. The saddest thing about the rush of our materialistic days is that they rob us of silence and communion with God. "The soul cannot be hurried." A less frantic pace is usually associated with the nurturing that love requires. The Lord Who gives the day *will* show the way if we ask Him. We assign ourselves an overload, but *never* does the Lord. If you are overloaded there is your answer right there. It is *not* God's will. *He will never assign you an overload.*

Answer these questions in your mind. What are the values that drive and shape your life? How do you decide between alternatives? How much does Christ have to say about your daily life and schedule? Who are you really, deep down inside? Have you ever asked yourself questions like that? There is no way to know ourselves unless we have time alone to explore. Most of us are trying to get *His* power to live out *our* commitments. We are asking Him to bless what we have already started. I accept a job and then say, "Lord, help me!" instead of asking in the beginning, "Lord, what is it you want me to do? Do you want me to accept this?"

The one thing I have tried to do recently that has helped me as much as any other one thing is *never* give someone an answer on the telephone. My first thought is *yes.* The hardest thing I ever say is *no.* Lately I have said, "Give me a little time to pray about it. Let me check it out with my husband. I will get back with you." I do not accept anything on the spot. As much as possible, respond to the demands of others on *your* schedule.

I have heard it said, "Anything we do without waiting for God's guidance and timing becomes a golden calf." We have instance after instance in the Scriptures of those who ran ahead of God. We just have to look at Sarah. She got impatient waiting for God, and tried to fix it. I don't think there is a mother who doesn't know about "fixing it." We want to fix everything for our children and grandchildren. We want to fix things for our husbands. It has taken me a long time to figure out *I can't fix everything.* My husband says, "Honey, you have done a good job of keeping four balls in the air [my children]. You cannot keep eight, ten, or twelve." I have finally faced up to that fact. My golden calf is probably my family, but all of us have one. When we pause in quiet and prayer we are inviting God into the holy place where the real decisions of life are made. Taking time to tune up is part of the solution to this age-old problem.

There are three possibilities. We can do what *we* want, keeping our lives under our direction and control. The second is we can do what *others* want, living up to all their expectations. Or we can do what *God* wants and pray in sincerity for His will to be done. I don't need to tell you which is correct.

JOURNAL ENTRY

I've never thought of myself as being the least bit creative. In fact, I have told it far and wide that there is *not* a creative bone in my body! I found out recently why. I was never *still* long enough. The Saints of old got their creativity from time alone with the Father. Out here on the breezeway has come to be my "special place" with *You*. Help me discover here the unique task You want me to do. I want to be *still* long enough for You to draw out of me that idea only I can do!

Creativity requires solitude, and modern life keeps us from daydreaming. Every moment of our day is squeezed by nonstop activity and we have little time for contemplation. Inspiration comes very slowly and quietly. The deep things of God have always been revealed in the secret places with the Most High. Meditation is part of the solution as He reveals to us the creativity He wants us to participate in.

I had an interior designer who worked with me and she said, "Anytime I do anything creative, I do it early in the morning before I am tired." Jesus was a morning person; read Mark 1:35. Imagine what it would do to your creativity and mine if we paused first thing upon rising, waiting for our instructions from the Lord. I read a good statement you might remember. "An ounce of morning is worth a pound of afternoon." Let's resolve to give the Lord the first fruits of our day, and then we can truly say, "For by His hand He leadeth me."

One of the reasons we fail to do this is *fear*. We don't know how

He is going to lead us or where. We fear opening ourselves up to God just as we fear opening ourselves up to other people. This is why we don't communicate in depth. We are not sure we want anybody to know everything about us. We are afraid if we pause with the Lord long enough He might ask us to do something we don't want to do. The same is true in discovering our spiritual gifts. It came as a surprise to me to realize some people don't want to know their gifts. I had always thought everybody would want to know how they are gifted. The rub is, once you find out your gifts, you must use them. If you don't want to use your gifts, there is less guilt if you don't know what they are.

Don't be afraid to ask the Lord His will. One author suggests, "The uneasiness we feel in quiet moments, our disquiet when all is quiet around us, our loneliness in a crowd, our deep insecurity when all seems outwardly in order, can press us back to God."

We have the illustration of the prodigal son. When he came to the end of his rope and was quiet, he returned to the Father. *The far country for you and me is anywhere we are away from God.* Some of us just need to return to the Father. When you put off the cares of the world, you can feel the everlasting arms. I don't know anything that slows me down like the thought of feeling the everlasting arms. Do you have a longing for God's direction? If not, ask Him to give you that "want to." He promised He would in Phil. 2:13: "For it is God which worketh in you both to will and to do of His good pleasure."

Someone said, "The older I become in the faith, the more impressed I am that the management of my time is the greatest spiritual barometer of my control by the Spirit." I think that is true. *Being busy is not a satisfactory substitute for being holy.* I have finally realized that my alone time is as essential to my spirit as food, sleep, and exercise are to my body.

I agree with Gigi G. Tchividjian, who said, "The Lord showed me that He was not to be found in a whirlwind of anxious activity, or in an earthquake of agitation, or in the fire of over commitment and busyness that so quickly consumes—but in gentle stillness."

JOURNAL ENTRY

I really feel like I'm walking a tightrope between overdo and underdo. I want to do enough to keep from *dwelling* on my problems, but I'm still trying to break my tendency from constant busyness. Help me find Your balance.

Schedule

We've discussed the *situation*. We've seen the *solution* from the Word of God and found it to be *solitude*. Now we must *schedule* proper priorities. Setting the right priorities is the first step toward holiness. The dictionary defines a priority as something being "first in rank, time or place, having first claim." Of course we know the Scripture says seek first the kingdom of God and His righteousness, and His promise is the supply of our needs.

Priorities are simply the choices you make about your use of time. Don't copy anyone's priorities. Yours will be unique. This is where we get in trouble. We have such a tendency to copy others. What we really need are blinders like those you see worn by horses. Your priorities are not going to be a carbon of anybody else's. They are unique for you just as you are a unique individual. Also they are going to be in a constant state of transition. My priorities now are not the same as when my four children were at home. They are not the same as they were last week, or the week before. They are in a constant state of change. The Lord leads us to make those adjustments as they need to be made, but it is your *choice* to follow Him.

Someone has said, "Priorities are the steering wheel, time management the tires of the vehicle to get you where you want to go." They keep one moving toward the fulfillment of one's purpose. A good thing for all of us to do is write down our life's purpose. Where do you want to be five years from now? What do you want to be ten years from now? Most of us have no idea where we are going.

The Bible does not give us a set of directions, but it does give us lots of clues. Think about some of these. If Jesus is our pattern, consider His life.

1) Jesus spent time alone with the Father. He always checked out the advice of men with His Heavenly Father.

2) He also had an intimate knowledge of the Scripture. Maybe this is where we need to begin. If you are not in a Bible study, get in one. One thing that keeps coming out in Scripture is the phrase

"the fullness of time." Jesus prayed and waited for orders. Again that is not our nature.

3) He also invested His life in people. Always put "people before things." Primarily Jesus made His investment in His disciples. He channeled most of His time and energy into these twelve men. I have channeled mine into my children. I trained my four, and now have an opportunity to influence my eight grandchildren. They are not my chief responsibility, but hopefully I can impact their lives in a positive way.

4) Christ was rarely portrayed as being in a hurry. Nowhere in Scripture do we find God to be rushing, hurrying, or hard pressed. The Bible says, "He walked in Galilee." "He sat on the hillside." You don't ever see Christ hurrying as we do, yet He did the will of the Father. From the cross He said, "It is finished."

5) He took breaks for restful leisure. He did not respond to every request. He even left the needs of people to spend time in prayer.

When I married a minister I told him, "You can tell that pulpit committee they are not getting two staff members for the price of one." Somewhere along the way, the Lord has changed my attitude and given me a new love for serving, teaching, and doing the things of the kingdom. Now I have the other problem. I don't want to say no to *anything*. However, I've learned there are times that I need to be quiet. Somebody has called it "sacred idleness." I like that. I used to feel that I was wasting time if I ever sat down. It helps to say, "I am engaged in sacred idleness!"

Paul said in Philippians, "This one thing I do." The power of direction is a dynamic force. Most worthwhile achievements are the result of many things supporting the ultimate aim.

The single-mindedness of Paul, I'm convinced, is the reason he experienced such *joy*. His main purpose was to glorify Jesus and to do the will of the Father. Ps. 108:1 says, "Oh God, my heart is fixed." We need to meditate long enough to know what He wants to do and then do this *one thing*.

Dwell on these things. Determine that today's rat race is going to get along with one less "rat"! Decide that some solitude is going to be a part of your schedule. Then *act* on what the Lord leads you to do. Stay at it—the rewards are tremendous.

Perhaps this modern version of the Twenty-third Psalm should be our guide:

> The Lord is my pace-setter—I shall not rush.
> He makes me stop for quiet intervals,
> He provides me with images of stillness which restore my serenity,
> He leads me in ways of efficiency through calmness of mind,
> And His guidance is peace.
> Even though I have a great many things to accomplish each day, I will not fret,
> For His Presence is here,
> His timelessness, His all importance, will keep me in balance.
> He prepares refreshment and renewal in the midst of my activity,
> By anointing my mind with His oils of tranquility,
> My cup of joyous energy overflows.
> Truly harmony and effectiveness shall be the fruits of my hours,
> For I shall walk in the Pace of my Lord
> And dwell in His House forever.

SOURCE UNKNOWN

PRAYER

Lord, I know serenity is a gift from You. Help me find that balance between overdo and underdo. Help me to operate my life serenely within Your cycle as faithfully as Your other handiwork.

Questions for Chapter 4

1) How does your present *situation* put stress on you and your family?

2) What *solutions* can you suggest that will help improve your current life-style?

3) Read the following Scriptures about *solitude:* Ps. 1:2, Zech. 2:13, Hab. 2:20. Now "be still and know that He is God."

CHAPTER 5

Journey to a Full Stop

FOR THOSE OF US blessed with impatient personalities, *W-A-I-T* is truly a four-letter word! "Tarrying," often referred to in Scripture, is irksome to say the least, and borders on the impossible for many of us. Yet I read, "God never says to us, 'Stand still, sit still or be still' unless He is going to do something." That thought intrigued me, as did this verse from Num. 9:19, "And when the cloud tarried . . . then the children of Israel kept the charge of the Lord and journeyed not."

Would that I had that kind of faith during periods of "divine waiting." We sing the familiar old hymn, "I'll go where You want me to go, dear Lord," when in reality His will may be for us to "stay where He wants us to stay."

Waiting for God! How difficult that is for those of us who want to charge ahead and take control of life! I still tend to think nothing is happening in my life unless I see *action*. However, during this crash course in "Waiting 101," I'm about to conclude that tarrying and remaining secluded seems to be the supreme test of obedience. As someone said, "*Submission* to the divine will is the softest pillow on which to recline." But, when our eyes are covered with blankets of limited understanding it is hard to remember that God is up to something!

JOURNAL ENTRY

". . . And He shall bring it to pass" (Ps. 37:5). Self-effort hinders His working when we insist on fighting our own battles, taking matters into our own hands. These are statements *so* characteristic of *me*. As someone said, "It seems so unsafe to just sit still, and do nothing but trust the Lord." It's like trying to save a drowning man who tries to help his rescuer—it is impossible. Our interference hinders His working. *Pray, really believe, wait, praise,* and *do* only what He says do!

In spite of my anxious spirit, impatient nature, and "do-it-yourself" attitude—I do want to *wait on You.* Just lead me unmistakably.

"The Waiting Game" is often played throughout life. It may be an emotional blackout caused by some disaster—loss of husband, child, job, or some injury. It may be a time of reassessment of our priorities. It may be a chance to select our way among the many choices that are available today, and to recover our balance. Or it may be, as mine was, a cessation of all activity when energy is "spent" and exhaustion has brought life to a halt.

What about you? Are you making progress or are undercurrents taking you away? Are you in a situation under a starless sky that drips darkness?

JOURNAL ENTRY

I can identify with this statement: "There are times I feel hopelessly buried under my own darkness, but never forget the God Who made us all is with us through every dusk and dawn." I'm so grateful for Your sure Presence that never leaves.

ANOTHER JOURNAL ENTRY

I found another *wonderful* promise today in Isa. 45:3—"And I will give thee the treasures of darkness, and hidden riches of secret places, that thou mayest know that I, the Lord, which call thee by thy name, am the God of Israel." When you are in the dark it is so hard to think about riches and treasures being there, but I have found that to be so.

How do we continue our journey? *We don't*—until the cloud clearly moves, we must "tarry." The phenomenal thing is that this period of waiting just may be a time of intense preparation for the next leg of the journey. I'm finding that to be true as this book is taking shape.

JOURNAL ENTRY

I feel I've been called aside for "a season" to learn some things. *Help me* now to be able to put those lessons in print to help others cope with the valleys and the shadows.

Corrie Ten Boom said, "Men have to go through many experiences in order to get the spiritual vision which is needed to see the divine plan. A film is developed in a darkroom." My problem continues to be wanting to fast-forward past the scary parts in my life instead of learning the hard way whatever it is the Lord is trying to teach me.

JOURNAL ENTRY

I feel just like I did as a little girl when Daddy and Mother were taking me to the mountains of North Georgia on vacation. I asked Daddy, "What are we going to *do*?" He said, "Rest!" I said, "But I'm not tired!"
I feel now You are telling me to *rest* when I'm not tired. How often we choose labor, when He says, "Rest."

I was reminded today that one can sin simply by refusing to wait. "To say *'Now!'* to God is as presumptuous as saying *'No!'*" Richard Halverson reminds us, "Submission to God's will includes submission to His schedule." Could it be that God allowed this crisis in my life to remind me that I never outgrow my need of Him?

Inevitable Delays

Irksome delays are often part of God's perfect planning. I learned this lesson well during the fall of 1990. Landrum and I had planned for some time to take *all* of our adult children to Israel. Since all four of our children are pastors or in church-related businesses, we felt this was the best thing we could give them to strengthen their walk with the Lord and enhance their ministries. With the decision made to "spend their inheritance," we set about planning this trip of a lifetime!
Leaving behind eight grandchildren was the first hurdle we

faced. Baby-sitters were no problem for David since he and Vicki were newly married and had not started their family. Roland and Lan were blessed enough to have precious in-laws willing to keep their kids, but Ann was not so fortunate. Finis's parents are both deceased and hers were making the trip!

The care of four children is an awesome responsibility at best, plus, at the time Ann was home-schooling, which meant it was a twenty-four-hour assignment. We had not come up with *any* satisfactory arrangement when the Persian Gulf War broke out. Even though Israel was never closed to tourists during that time, our family "troops" became restless!

We wavered back and forth between going and not going. At one point, most of the boys wanted to go on without the girls since they were the most apprehensive. We had hoped the trip would strengthen their marriages and not destroy them so we decided to cancel the trip and go at a later time.

My disappointment was perhaps the most severe. I'm worse than a kid when my plans go awry. Once we had gotten the consent of everybody, which was no small feat, I could not understand these circumstances. In my usual lack of faith, I questioned the Lord as to why?

I put the pieces together in the months that unfolded, and as usual, *He* turned what I thought was bad into good. The trip was to have been in November, and my October illness would have made it impossible for me to make the jaunt, and at that late date no refund of deposits would have been given.

As it turned out, we were able to go the next year when nobody had to be anxious over the world situation. By that time, Ann had moved to Cameron, Texas, and the Lord provided *great* care for her children. There was a couple in her church willing to take on that assignment who had been house parents for the Texas Baptist Children's Home. With that background, we felt confident they could handle her four! The Lord's timing truly is *perfect*.

I keep reminding myself God is still on His throne and even delay is part of His goodness. I also keep reminding myself that others have survived waiting periods. Think about it—most of the Psalms were born in difficulty. We find in chapter 27:13-14: "I would have despaired, unless I had believed that I would see the goodness of the Lord in the land of the living. Wait for the Lord;

Be strong, and let your heart take courage; yes, wait for the Lord!" (NAS).

A precious friend wrote me during my illness: "Although I've never been in your shoes, my heart goes out to you. It's not easy to adjust when the Lord changes our direction, but I know, somehow, *He* will see you through." She also sent me the words to the song Larnelle Harris sings so beautifully:

> It's not in trying but in trusting,
> It's not in running but in resting,
> Not in wondering but in praying
> that we find the strength of the Lord.

The Reality Process

Slowly but surely, I seem to be making my way through the grief process. *Denial*—"I didn't have a stroke." *Bargaining*—"Lord, I'll do anything—just don't take away what I love doing best." *Anger*—there seemed to be no immediate answers. *Depression*—guilt and anger turned inward; that feeling of helplessness and hopelessness when life has lost its joy. The final stage is *acceptance.*

If I am going to receive the greatest benefit from my wilderness experience, I must *accept* my situation and learn from it. This giving up of self-will is the hardest thing we human beings are ever called on to do. Chances are that the life I once knew is *never* going to be again, but "fretting" just adds another problem. Resentment and bitterness develop when we persist in resisting what God has allowed to happen to us. If we are living self-centered lives and something happens to disrupt our carefully laid plans, our natural tendency is to react with impatience and resentment. Resentment can compound physical pain and leave us with embittered personalities, and I surely don't want that to happen to me. They say the impatient horse that will not quietly endure his halter only strangles himself in his stall. I finally have faced the fact that I have been strangling myself by wanting my own way, and by not accepting the fact that I will never be able to do all I once did.

JOURNAL ENTRY

I've got to practice the "letting go" prayer of thoughts and other things beyond my control. Help me surrender my feelings, my emotions, health, family, future, schedule, book—*all* to You.

I'm told, "Half our trouble comes from wanting to have our own way, and the other half is due to failure to face the facts." It is in knowledge of the genuine conditions of our lives that we must draw our strength to live and our reasons for living. The good news is that "the capacity for knowing God enlarges as we are brought by Him into circumstances which oblige us to exercise faith." Christians grow as we accept whatever God allows to enter our lives, and we seldom grow apart from "no way out" situations.

This has been a time of what Kay Arthur calls "porch sitting"—a new experience for me. I keep being reminded there is no time lost in such waiting hours. Charles H. Spurgeon said, "Delayed answers to prayer are not only trials of faith, but they give us opportunities of honoring God by our steadfast confidence in Him under apparent repulses."

Sometimes the Lord calls us aside for a "season."

JOURNAL ENTRY

March 20—First day of *spring*. It is so easy to always rush each season—to be winter-weary and summer-hungry! However, it is when the death of winter has done its work that the sun can draw out in each plant its own individuality and make its existence full and fragrant. I find myself rushing over this "slowed down" season of my life, too. Help me choose beauty and faith over understanding. Thank You, Lord, for the seasons of life—sunshine after storms, rainbows after strife.

I feel like the little boy in *Children's Letter to God*. He said, "I keep waiting for spring but it never came yet. Don't forget" (Mark).

When our souls are barren in a winter that seems hopeless and endless, God has not abandoned us. The Son is always behind the cloud! He asks our acceptance of the painful parts and our realization that for every winter of our lives, as long as we don't give up, as long as we truly believe in God and in ourselves, there will always be a spring. The winter snow lies long, but it goes at last!

JOURNAL ENTRY

I wrote in my family letter yesterday that this spring had particular significance for me as I saw the azaleas and the new growth on the trees. I'm reminded the Lord is still in charge of new life, new beginnings, and for flowers to once again bloom. After this barren time of illness in my life, I'm trusting the Lord to bring new life and sparkle to me once again. I'm so grateful I know the Great Physician!

I remember well the occasional snow or ice storm when we lived in Texas. Meetings would be canceled, schools closed, and we would play with our children, eat chili by the fire, and get some much-needed rest. I still have a smart-aleck friend who calls me every time it snows and says, "I've got the chili on, where are you?!"

We invariably commented during those times that since we didn't have sense enough to slow down, the Lord would just immobilize us. We thanked Him for those times when we could *enjoy* the fire, but we chafe under the wait when we think the fire threatens to consume us and we cannot see any good in our experience.

It is so easy to trust the Lord when the sun is shining, but let the storm come and we doubt. We seem to equate blessing only with the goodness of God. Not so—trials filtered through His omnipotent fingers of love can just make us more like Jesus.

My favorite words have become "this too shall pass." Storms do pass, clouds do clear, and sunshine is always on the other side. Faith is not denying the weather that sweeps over our lives. It's believing that behind the clouds and beyond the storms waits a faithful God.

JOURNAL ENTRY

I read again Ps. 27 about *waiting*. The promise I claimed was verse 13—"I am still confident of this: I will see the goodness of the Lord in the land of the living" (NIV®).

ANOTHER JOURNAL ENTRY

> I still get impatient with my slow improvement. Swindoll says, "Not a one of us finds a delay easy to accept, but our faith is fleshed out at times like this."
>
> Anybody can walk in victory when all is going well, but the ability to accept delay or disappointment graciously has got to come from You. I guess that is why patience is listed as a "fruit of the Spirit" (Gal. 5:22-23).

We so often equate silence with separation, but Rom. 8 assures us of the fallacy of that thought. Some good advice I received and have tried to practice is: "*Seek not* too soon to disapprove His work! To suspend judgment when God is silent honors Him because it refuses to charge Him with being unjust."

Those who bless God *in* their trials will be blessed by God *through* their trials. The tendency is always to ask, "Why?" Seeking answers is not necessarily wrong. In fact, one doctor told me there is no such thing as a bad question. If we completely neglect looking for answers, it may show how little interest we have in our situation or that of another. Any question that brings us to God for an answer is a *good* question. It is okay to wrestle with God about the questions that perplex us—just be sure to stop talking long enough to *listen!* I read in *Open Windows,* "If I stop asking, I give up on any expectation that things can be better. In seeking answers, I continue to rely on belief in God in Whose hands are my life."

I *do* think my part of acceptance is giving up my "right" to understand why (I may have reason, but no "right" . . .) and waiting for the reasons until afterward. The evidence isn't all in yet, and the verdict has not been pronounced. Instead of asking God a lot of questions, look up and lay hold of His assurances. The future is in God's hands and our job is simply to wait—claiming the promise: "But they that wait upon the Lord shall renew their strength" (Isa. 40:31). "Since the Lord is directing our steps, why try to understand everything that happens?" (Prov. 20:24 TLB).

"Waiting with hope changes one's perspective on the problems of living in difficult circumstances," says Roger Crook, a professor at Meredith College.

Suffering becomes discipline.
Endurance becomes perseverance.

Fear becomes confident expectation.

Anxiety becomes confidence.

Disappointment becomes satisfaction.

Crook says, "The problems of the present are no less real, but they are seen as part of a much broader whole."

JOURNAL ENTRY

"Humble yourselves, therefore, under the mighty hand of God, that He may exalt you in due time" (1 Pet. 5:6). Help me to trust that in Your timing I can be renewed, and my strength will return.

I have faced the fact that God may have allowed my problems to get my attention. There is nothing like utter bankruptcy to help us recognize the importance of our *Helper.* If I look on this period as *His* training, then I must conclude there aren't any shortcuts—no detours around the valleys. We usually mature in our faith walk *only* as we pass through fiery trials and tests. I continue to be reminded that "there has never been known great saintliness of soul which did not pass through great suffering." Invariably, those who have been used of God most in public have gone through deep waters in secret.

JOURNAL ENTRY

I'm finding so many encouragements in my reading: "Blessed are ye if ye trust, where ye cannot understand." Also— "He has attained to an eminent degree of Christian grace who know how to *wait.*"

From a practical standpoint, how do you wait? I'll suggest three, not so simple, ways.

1) *Wait in prayer.* When we consult God, we are humbling ourselves, seeking His will and guidance. Lack of prayer is nothing but subtle pride.

JOURNAL ENTRY

I read today where Hezekiah prayed and "spread it before

the Lord." That's what I'm doing today—I don't feel good. My
head is spinning, and I'm concerned again. What do I do now?
Give me stamina to go on, courage to stop, or whatever it is
You want me to do. I honestly don't know. *Help me.*

When God's people pray, I know He delights in providing. So my
job is to wait quietly until it pleases Him to answer. Ps. 42:11 says,
"Expect God to act" (TBL), and *I'm expecting.*

JOURNAL ENTRY

Delays are not refusals—God has a set time as well as a set
purpose. He will set the time of our deliverance. Help me not
to be depressed by the enforced rest, but use it for prayer and
contemplation.

2) *Wait in faith.* "Thy budding plans are in Thy Father's holding."
Express unwavering confidence in Him. No matter how near the
precipice He may take you, don't snatch the reins out of His hand.
There is no such thing as a problem that doesn't have a gift in it.
The question is, will you choose to trust God even if He never
allows you to know why He has allowed a tragedy to enter your life?
3) *Wait in quiet patience.* Never murmur; accept the case. We *can*
arrive at a place where nothing can upset or disturb our calm. Paul
did, and I pray for that—a constant calm within! It won't come
until all my striving ceases. That's my job! Trust God to adjust your
tangled life and bring His will. F. B. Meyer said, "You must be
brought to the end of yourself before God can begin with you."
If you have a problem you can't solve, turn the matter over to
Him. He has promised to make the crooked pieces straight and to
unwind all the snarls (see Isa. 45:2). Life is like a puzzle. Why is it
we don't hand these puzzling situations over to our loving heavenly
Father?

JOURNAL ENTRY

I confess to being impatient with God's delays—it is so hard
to "*walk* with God" when my pace had been what it was. I've

learned the truth of this statement—Patience is a virtue that carries a lot of *wait!*

Billy Graham suggests still another step in the grief process and that is *acceptance with joy.* This is when we accept the process, quit fighting God, and give over our self-will to each of life's "episodes" as they unfold. Acceptance with joy says, "This is my situation at the moment and I'll accept willingly whatever a loving heavenly Father sends."

JOURNAL ENTRY

Last night in our New Year's Eve service the pastor asked us to make one wish or prayer for the New Year. Mine was, as I know my heart, to do Your will—whatever that is. I've lived with this fear of a stroke or dying this last year, but I tried to pray as earnestly as I know how—"For me to live is Christ, to die is gain." It's Your call—give me the grace to accept it.

I'm reminded of the song:

Dear Lord and Father of Mankind,
Drop Thy still dews of quietness,
till all our strivings cease;
take from our soul the strain and stress,
and let our ordered lives
confess the beauty of Thy peace.

Waiting expresses dependence upon God and brings quietness to the soul. We must choose. Each individual must decide for himself whether he walks in God's ways or not! If you are facing insurmountable problems and feel that you are on the precipice of panic, call to mind that our heavenly Father acts for the one who waits for Him. "For since the world began no one has seen or heard of such a God as ours, who works for those who wait for Him" (Isa. 64:4 TLB). Victory comes to those who turn from the indecision of shaking on the premises to the joy of standing on the promises of God.

PRAYER

O Lord, in our television-indoctrinated culture where crimes are committed and solved in twenty-eight minutes, we have become addicted to the instantaneous solution. Help us, Father, to take the long look, to see things in perspective, and give me patience to grow in the darkness. Help me to replace my "what if?" fears with Your promises.

Questions for Chapter 5

1) Has your life ever come to a stop? What did you learn while waiting?

2) How do you respond to those inevitable delays in life? What changes will you make in the future?

3) Read Ps. 27. What does David say to you about waiting?

CHAPTER 6

Journey among Family

DON'T MISS THE JOY of a close family! I have confessed on other occasions to being a "family nut." There are eighteen of us now. We are beginning to look like the TV "Waltons." Somebody said about our recent Christmas card, "Next year it is going to be an album!"

After my confidence about getting through this book and having faith, my third certainty is the importance of family. I have four children, and had they not been by Caesarean section I might have fallen into Grandmother Leavell's footsteps, who had nine boys! Suffice it to say, I would have made a real good Catholic!

My family has been a source of tremendous comfort during my wilderness experience. I hope you understand that your family is your *greatest* earthly possession. Make your family life a priority. It won't take but one experience like mine to realize how "special" they are. When Ann called my husband and told him I was in the hospital in Baton Rouge, he came. He canceled preaching—something he had never done before. I really thought I was dying! His attitude was, "Mom, we are going to get through this together. Whatever this is, we are going to see it through." I fell in love with him all over again.

My daughter stayed right by my side. Her precious husband kept their four children to enable her to spend the nights with me. At the time, I thought that was so unnecessary and told her so. However, the very next week in that same hospital a woman was raped. I said, "Thank You, Lord. Thank you, Ann, for spending those nights with me."

You would have to know Lan, my Phoenix son, to appreciate this statement but he called everybody we had ever known. I said, "Lan, did you have to tell *everybody?*" His response was, "Mom, I have got you covered in prayer." How do you argue with that? I just wanted to hug him.

My middle son, Roland, sent me *gorgeous* flowers. I first credited Lisa, my sweet daughter-in-law who is so precious, with that thoughtful gesture. However, she said, "Mom, I did not send those flowers. Roland did." She said he had told her, "I've got to send my mama some flowers." Wasn't she a dear to share that with me?

David, our youngest son, pastored close to Baton Rouge. He and his wife, Vicki, came as soon as possible. There is nothing like family when you need them. They are the most precious possessions we have and a real source of strength in hard times. Take care of your family and make them a priority. You will never regret the time you spend with them. The love you give *will* return tenfold!

In July of 1990 I did something I had never done before. I responded to a request from *Good Housekeeping Magazine* for letters from full-time homemakers. This request came on the heels of First Lady Barbara Bush's commencement address at Wellesley College. Some students had picketed before her appearance, stating they felt her identity was her husband's and not her own since she had never worked outside the home.

I remember becoming *livid* when I read that newspaper account, so I felt compelled to write a letter when the opportunity came for full-time moms to have equal time. I sent the following letter, which expresses my conviction about the importance of the home and family.

July 23, 1990

GOOD HOUSEKEEPING
959 Eighth Avenue
New York, New York 10019
ATTN: Articles Dept. C.K.

Dear Sirs:

I read with interest your appeal for letters from full-time homemakers. I decided to respond since I speak as a satisfied customer of that profession. It may seem strange to some to speak of homemaking as a "profession," but many others who have chosen a similar route will understand that terminology.

Homemaking was a *choice* for me. I finished college with a degree which fully prepared me to enter the work force. Contrary to opinions of some, I "chose" full-time mothering, and I have found my own identity in that calling. Some would have you believe "identity" comes only on the first and the fifteenth with a paycheck. Not so—mine has come as I have watched my four children mature into responsible adults, join caring professions, and establish Christian homes of their own.

You asked, "What are the worst—and best—moments I have experienced in this role?" The worst side of parenting probably has to do with those sleepless nights when you lie awake wondering if your values are going to be those of your teenage son or daughter. Parenting was not problem-free for us, but we claimed the biblical promise, "Train up a child in the way he should go; and when he is old, he will not depart from it" (Proverbs 22:6).

At this writing our children are all happily married. We have added a daughter-in-law and precious grandchild since the enclosed picture was taken bringing our family total now to eighteen.

I hope the best part of life for me will always be the present. Now that my active days of mothering are over, I have moved into other areas of interest. I teach, have just had my first book published, and speak frequently to women's groups. Guess what I tell them? I urge them to be a full-time Mom! "I have no greater joy than to hear that my children walk in truth" (John 4).

I agree with First Lady Barbara Bush who is reported to have said at Wellesley College, "At the end of your life, you will never regret not having passed one more test, not winning one more verdict, or not closing one more deal. You *will* regret time not spent with a husband, a child, a friend, or a parent."

Sincerely,
Mrs. Landrum P. Leavell

I immediately sent a copy of this letter to my four children, and was thrilled at their response. Not until later did I find out my daughter and daughter-in-law had written the following letters.

GOOD HOUSEKEEPING
959 Eighth Avenue
New York, New York 10019
ATTN: Articles Dept. C.K.

Dear Sirs:

In the mail today I received from my mother a copy of a letter she wrote to you in response to your appeal for letters from full-time homemakers. I decided that I would write to you as well and give you "the rest of the story. . . ."

I too have *chosen* homemaking! I also finished college with a degree in business administration. My parents taught me that this was the best insurance policy in case I was ever widowed and left to raise children on my own. I pray that never happens because I *love* being a stay-at-home mom.

I am 33 years old and like my mother have four children. No occupation could ever rival the one I enjoy today. To be there for every first smile and first step, as well as the final stitches, is something I wouldn't trade even for a six figure salary—ever! I have taken one step further my parents' biblical promise, "Train up a child in the way he should go; and when he is old, he will not depart from it" (Proverbs 22:6). I teach my children at home. I have a third and first grader as well as two preschoolers. This is by far the most rewarding part of mothering I've experienced!

What my mom didn't tell you in her letter was that not only have I, her only daughter, chosen homemaking as a career, but her three daughters-in-law as well. I am convinced that it was her excellent example and "training" that made this profession something to be desired rather than endured and something that my brothers would seek in a mate.

So not only do I love and respect my mom, but I have the honor of following her in *the* greatest career that any woman could ever have!

Sincerely,
Mrs. Finis Beauchamp

GOOD HOUSEKEEPING
959 Eighth Ave
New York, New York 10019
ATTN: Articles Dept. C.K.

Dear Sirs:

Not to be outdone by my sister-in-law, I decided to give an "out-law" point of view. I, too, have chosen to be a wife and mother at home.

My mother was a homemaker until she had to support two children in college, so I had her as an example, as well as my mother-in-law. I always wanted to raise my own children— teaching them respect, values, morals, trust, and to live a Christian life. I didn't want to leave these virtues to someone else. My husband and I waited six years before we had children. I worked all this time, making sure we were ready and willing to take the full responsibility and challenge of child rearing. After two miscarriages, I was more than ready! This made my children even more special! I'm glad we waited, but I wouldn't trade being a mother for any worldly possession!

I have a two year old, and a one year old. When I decided to have them, I did it in one swoop! I don't believe I'm as tough as my sister-in-law, so I won't have four children, but my two are adored and spoiled!

My husband and I decided we could do without lots of things, just so I could sit home with our children. *They* are what's important, *things* are not.

Yet, I had a wonderful example in my own mother. She was always there when I needed her—even before I needed her! She took care of three children, was always involved in PTA, had many church activities, but always had meals cooked and our clothes washed and ironed. I don't know if she ever slept! And she raised responsible, moral, Christian children.

My mother-in-law raised four wonderful children, too, so I'm certain she did an excellent job in her "calling" for life. I can't think of any other family I'd rather be a part of. I LOVE being a Leavell! So much so, that I wrote a poem when my sister-in-law, Susanne, joined the clan in 1985. She, now, feels the same way I do.

I hope being a housewife "begets" being a housewife. I want my own daughter to experience this joy! I do hope and pray

that I do as well with my children as my "parents"—both sets—
have done with theirs.

Sincerely,
Lisa Leavell

TO: Susanne Gentry Leavell
FROM: Lisa Rives Leavell

Becoming a Leavell is more than a name change;
It's a home change,
A heart change,
But even more strange . . .
It's loving and giving
And giving some more.
It's hoping and waiting to see what's in store.
It's going and doing
And trying what's new
While keeping a grip on what's tried and what's true.
It's a name full of history,
A family of pride,
For in every heart the Lord doth abide,
From California to China,
From Annie to you,
The background is there but there's still much to do.
There are people to meet
And places to see.
There are footsteps to follow
And so much to be.
We cling to each other
For strength and for love,
Knowing it came first from the Father above.
For God so loved us that He sent us His Son
To die for our sins that the world may be won.
Winning the world is the Leavell Clan's Creed
In all that you say,
Your life and your deed.
So it's not just the name that you soon will gain.
It's a life worth the living
And not one in vain.
So prepare to be different,

To be surprised,
To be pleased,
And be thankful to God every night on your knees
That in this one life you were divinely blessed.
You're becoming a Leavell;
You're becoming the best.

I never saw any follow-up in the magazine from that request, but it may have been because they were inundated with mail from the Leavell family! However, this sums up our strong commitment to the family.

I think you might find it interesting to hear from my husband and family concerning my illness. The following is my husband's response to my illness.

Landrum's Response

Telephone calls have great potential for good or bad. I had no reason for anxiety or apprehension when the phone rang that Saturday morning, October 27, 1990. I have never liked for Jo Ann to travel alone in the car, but some of my resistance to her driving alone had disappeared with the coming of car phones! However, this call was not from the car, nor was Jo Ann on the other end.

Little did I know the changes in our lives that would take place in the next year or so following "the call." It was our daughter, Ann, calling. I felt good about that arrangement for the weekend, with Ann sharing the room with her mother. She started off with an effort not to alarm me, saying something to the effect that everything was fine, but that she and mother were in the emergency room at Our Lady of the Lake Hospital. She urged me not to hurry or worry, but thought I needed to move in that direction A.S.A.P. It took a few seconds to sink in, then I began to mobilize. My suitcase was already packed to drive to Pensacola, Florida, that afternoon, where I was interim pastor of the Olive Baptist Church.

In short order I was in the car and moving with total disregard for the laws of the State of Louisiana. I was fortunate enough to have been driving at a time when no troopers were patrolling I-10, and I set a new record for the trip. My mind was racing much faster than my car, and based on the meager information I had, there was wide latitude for speculation and "what ifs." I found that my mind went quickly to the worst case scenario, which tended to increase the miles per hour and loosen the tear ducts.

Please understand that I did not marry a neurotic or a whiner. Jo Ann's worst ailments have been a common cold that would turn into a cough, and having a baby once in a while. All four kids were born by Caesarean section, and she would be walking the next day! She had also had a hysterectomy and four invasive biopsies, but these were about like having the hiccups for her. She was always in good health, walked several miles a day, and had never had a need for even mild medication. Her personal schedule was at one speed—wide open! This did not begin when she became a pastor's wife, but was true when I met her. With her schedule and mine, we had to work really hard to get in our dates. I picked her up at nine o'clock at night many times, when she got out of class at Tulane. Some of our dates on Sunday nights were at 11:00 P.M., when I drove in from my church. That only gave us time for a hamburger and an orange freeze at Camellia Grill, since midnight was her curfew.

When I got to the hospital, I found the emergency room and the little cubicle where she and Ann were. Jo Ann was sitting up, smiling, and greeted me with a big kiss. I think I can safely say she had never been happier to see me! Both girls began to fill in the details of the last two hours or so. Even then the hand of God became increasingly incredibly clear.

The neurologist who was on call was believed by many to be the finest in the city, and he immediately ordered a series of tests. Shortly after my arrival he came in, and I was all ears and had a hundred questions. All her vital signs were normal, and he was puzzled. The natural explanation was a light stroke, causing numbness, but this was not indicated by blood pressure, heart rate, etc. Consequently, the testing would continue and Dr. Gold said she probably needed to stay another day or two. My question was whether or not I could bring her to Southern Baptist in New Orleans, where we were familiar with the facilities and knew the physicians. It was irritating to me when he opined that she would get better medical and hospital care there than in New Orleans. I decided not to get in a hassle with him, or even tell him I was on the Board of Directors at Baptist in New Orleans! Jo Ann did get good attention, but it was probably just a tad below what she could have gotten in New Orleans.

They did all the standard tests and a few exotic ones. The results were all negative, or inconclusive, and with each report I began to feel better, becoming convinced that it was not a threatening health problem.

I had called Pensacola and they assured me they could take care of the three services, nor did I have to worry about commuting from New Orleans, since Ann and Finis lived within a few miles of the hospital. God continued to supply our needs, and the other seminary administrators proved again that the seminary could do well without me, thank you!

In an overall view of the situation, I felt good about the future at that point. Jo Ann felt good, was up and walking around, and the numbness had left her hand and arm. I was looking forward to her release, and our return to the seminary and home. Little did I know what the coming months held.

Upon departure from the Baton Rouge hospital, we were sternly charged with the responsibility of getting her under the care of a neurologist in New Orleans. A neurologist was recommended, whom I knew, and even though all the tests and X rays from Baton Rouge were brought to New Orleans, these did not seem to be acceptable in New Orleans. The process started all over, with EEGs, EKGs, CAT scans, MRIs, angiogram, and others.

Jo Ann became increasingly disturbed, wondering what they were looking for. When direct questions were asked, only evasive answers came. More than one time during those weeks Jo Ann asked me, in tears, if I knew something that I wasn't telling her. Though I affirmed repeatedly that she knew everything I knew, she wasn't satisfied because the tests continued. I don't recall the exact sequence, but we got an appointment with a kind, godly internist whom we both knew. He seemed to understand her plight, and expressed concern over the way both the neurosurgeon and the neurologist had responded. He called both of these other doctors, talked with them numerous times, and tried to interpret to Jo Ann what they had said. The problem was they didn't know what the problem was!

The internist recommended a cardiologist, who gave a glimmer of understanding of the situation. He ran more tests and gave his diagnosis: Jo Ann had mitral valve prolapse, and carpal tunnel syndrome in her wrists and hands.

His explanation made sense. The heart valve had thickened, would not close completely, and he believed an infinitesimal clot had formed, broken loose, and gone to the brain. This caused the slightly irregular brain wave. The clot could have gone anywhere else in the body and would never have been heard of. It happened to go to the brain. The reoccurring tingling in Jo Ann's hands, especially at night, was a circulation problem caused by carpal tunnel syndrome. Neither of these was a life-threatening problem, but a life-style-threatening matter. This was glorious good news, but it came late for Jo Ann.

By the time this diagnosis was made, the six or seven months of concern, fear, anxiety, uncertainty, and sleeplessness had taken their toll. She was in the depths of full-scale depression, for she had faced the specter of brain tumors (seven EEGs), cancer, the threat of other and perhaps paralyzing strokes, becoming an invalid, and the possibility of having to give up all the things she loved so well: teaching her class of ministers' wives, teaching her interdenominational Bible study for ladies, speaking at women's conferences across the country, cooking and homemaking, and innumerable other things. She had to deal with her own finitude for the first time, for I am confident she had spent very little time previously entertaining the thought of dying.

Every one of these maladies and others also were running through my mind, but the big difference was that the illness was not happening to me. You can be assured I faced the possibility of life without Jo Ann, and all I could pray was, "Lord, You know how I need her, how dependent I am on her, and how useless I'd be without her." At that time we had been married thirty-eight years, and the bonding was complete—we had become "one flesh." It never occurred to me that I might be left alone. I had assumed that Jo Ann would be a widow and outlive me. The averages point out that wives live longer than their husbands. I could have made myself sick if I had focused on the bad things that could happen, but I was certain that she needed me healthy more than ever before.

The first obvious step in recovery for Jo Ann was the growing length of time between tears. Having never been emotional, I knew how bad she must have been feeling when, in silence, her chin would tremble and the tears would fall. It was a totally helpless feeling for me, and all I knew to do was hug and kiss! I had concluded that all I was capable of doing was to provide a support system for my best gal and pal. If the doctors couldn't figure it out, it certainly was beyond my capacity.

I rearranged my preaching schedule so I only went to the places I could drive, and she could go with me. I kept my office schedule flexible so I could take her to her doctors' appointments, and be there to hear any recommendations they made. Some of the doctors proved to be as inscrutable and noncommunicative with me as they were with her! I got a good grip on her disenchantment with certain of the medical profession. It is my belief that some of them simply cannot confess, "I do not know!"

The recovery was slow, and at times imperceptible, but it has continued. We are to the point that stressful times still give her "funny feelings" in her head, but fellow sufferers of mitral valve prolapse say this is a normal symptom, and one has to accept it and live with it. I believe that Jo Ann has accepted that, but still has some frustrations and discontent with not feeling exactly the way she did for her first fifty-nine years.

What are the lessons I have learned?

1) Life is fragile. Who can know what a day will bring?

2) Doctors and tests have their limitations. Only Jesus is omniscient.

3) Friends and loved ones are blessings beyond description—there is no way adequately to thank a host of people who were there when we needed them. For instance, my sister, Margaret, came during our annual trustee meeting and served as hostess for all the festivities at a time when Jo Ann couldn't bear being around people and having to talk! Carol Corvin "adopted" Jo Ann and was always available to drive her to the doctor's office, hospital, or do what was needed.

4) God really doesn't ever leave us or forsake us. He really does give His peace when we reach human extremity and put our weakness in His loving, caring hands.

Family's Response

I also invited my children to share the feelings they remember in the hopes it might help others when the lives of their loved ones are threatened. Just as a mother "bleeds" when her children are cut, inevitably each person will suffer in some way when someone he/she loves is hurt or sick. Being interdependent people, we do not have emotional highs and lows in a vacuum. Others are directly affected too.

This is a copy of the letter I sent them:

> Dear Children of Mine,
>
> I'm going to ask you a special favor. Maybe the week after Christmas when things are usually a little quiet, you can think about it.
>
> It probably won't come as any great surprise, but I'm writing another book entitled *Joy in the Journey*. It will mainly be about my little "episode," and some lessons learned through it all. I thought it might be helpful to others going through "fire" experiences.
>
> We never suffer alone; others are always affected. Daddy wrote his feelings (included), and I'm asking you to write anything you remember from those days from a child's perspective—how you felt, what thoughts crossed your mind, lessons learned, etc. Be as transparent as possible since I've become increasingly convinced that is how we minister best to others.
>
> It doesn't have to be long or involved—just your feelings. Nothing very "learned" could go in my simple book. Make it a "team effort" if you like, and include any input from my children-in-love. How about getting it to me sometime in January. Okay? I will appreciate it!
>
> Luv, Mom

I'm going to take excerpts from their responses in the order in which I received them.

Roland's perspective

As usual, messages are relayed to me through my wife and I faintly remember the surprise I experienced when Lisa notified me that Ann had taken you to the hospital in Baton Rouge. For some reason it was very difficult to picture you sick as throughout my twenty-two years of growing up under your roof, I don't recollect ever seeing you take an aspirin. I guess for that reason it is difficult to picture people who are never sick experiencing illness and you feel inadequate trying to comfort them during the illness out of lack of experience.

Over the succeeding months I experienced significant frustration in not ever knowing exactly what was wrong with you. For probably six or eight months I blamed it on you and Dad because throughout the years we have never known anything about your physical condition, and we were always the last to know when there were physical problems experienced. Even what could have been the gravest of problems were always written off as very insignificant. Upon reflection, it has become evident that part of the reason that we did not get any more information than we did is because you didn't have any information to give.

Over the months we were repeatedly told that you were going back and forth for additional tests and we had no idea whether or not the problems were much more significant than we were being told. Being left in the dark, we probably drew a lot of false conclusions with regard to the seriousness of your condition. In hindsight, I can understand now that you were in the same position not knowing much more than we did.

If my memory serves me correctly, it was around Christmas of 1991 when we were notified of the depression that you experienced on the backside of this illness. Never having experienced depression, and being three hours away from you, it was hard for me to even know what you were feeling.

Having never faced the prospect of death directly, it is hard for me to understand how well I would have responded if I were in your situation. Since I fly for a living there is never a time that I sit down in an airplane that I don't think of prospects of death and how it would affect my family, my business, and everything else that I would leave behind. It is from this perspective that I have resolved to enjoy what I do in business, enjoy the time that I spend with my family, and not dedicate all of my resources to retirement days. I have chosen to make a commitment to enjoying each day and each year that we live.

Lisa and I reflected over the holidays of 1992 how lucky we are to have both sets of our parents still living and in her case even a grandmother is still alive.

An additional benefit to both of us is the fact that we had the privilege of growing up in families where we were solidly led by Christian parents. Neither of us has any apprehension with regard to the fact that we will enjoy our eternal reward in heaven with our earthly parents.

Presently, a lady in our office has a sister-in-law in ICU, a son who had emergency surgery last night, and a father-in-law who is expecting surgery for cancer within the next ten days. It is at select times in our lives that we recognize the fragile nature of life on this earth and take the opportunity to recommit ourselves to service of our Lord. How quickly illness can bring us to the realization that the only legacy that we leave behind is the legacy of our children and the influence that we have held over other people's lives for the cause of Christ.

You asked for my comments, and feeble as they are, you have them.

Love, Roland

David's perspective

Crisis has a way of mending, healing, and fortifying relationships or repelling individuals further away than they have ever been. Through Mom's ordeal, our family has been brought closer together. As a family, we enjoy joking and kidding each other. People who aren't familiar with our family may even be shocked by "our ways" (examples: Lisa and Vicki). When the chips are down, like in an emergency situation, the kidding and joking stop and we band together. As my mom says, "We close ranks when something happens to one of us." Two instances come to mind related to this incident.

One dealt with Mom and Ann. They have always had a bond that was close. In our home, the females had to stick together because they were a minority. There were only two of them (if you don't include Tina, our dog!). Ann and Mom were together the whole weekend for this conference where Mom was speaking. When the "episode" happened, Ann was there to help Mom and take her to the hospital. She called Dad. She stayed in the hospital, and assisted in every conceivable way. It was providential that she and Finis lived in Port Allen, Louisiana, and was with Mom when the "episode" happened. I think that the time they spent together served as a "bonding" time.

Vicki and I received a phone call from Dad on October 27, 1990, informing us that Mom had been admitted to the hospital in Baton Rouge. We were in the middle of a cookout for our Sunday School class. As soon as we could get everyone out the door, we packed up the car and headed two hours to the hospital.

Mom always tries to give the appearance of being in control! I guess that it is some kind of matriarchal complex. Even in a hospital bed, this day was no different. We spent the afternoon with her in the hospital and then returned to Bogalusa, Louisiana, for our Sunday responsibilities.

The second instance concerns Mom and me. During the days, weeks, and months following the "episode," I was the only child who was in New Orleans on a regular basis. I was attending the New Orleans Baptist Theological Seminary pursuing a Ph.D. degree. During those days I began to be able to read some of Mom's signals. She had good days and bad days, and I became proficient at being able to tell how she was feeling (even over the telephone!). That bothered Mom because she didn't want anyone to know that she wasn't feeling well. As Dad said in his recounting of this story, Mom was used to running at 150 percent. Now she was being forced to run at 60 percent-75 percent. That frustrated her immensely. To tell her that she wasn't telling you the truth when she said she was fine was even more frustrating for her! I remember telling her that one day. Her chin started quivering and those crocodile tears started rolling off her cheeks. I hugged her and told her that it was okay to not feel good. Everyone has days that are worse than others.

Mom had never dealt with finitude. Not being able to accomplish something that she put her mind to was something that she had never experienced. This illness was the first such instance in her life from which she couldn't bounce back quickly. Although this drove her to depression, this added a "real" dimension to Mom. She was no longer immortal, unconquerable, or "able to jump small buildings in a single bound." In the long run, it added a new dimension to her personality that assisted in her ability to minister to others. At times she still deals with the "immortal complex" (by the way, she is a Leavell!) but she is handling it with grace and growing in Christ through it all. It is exciting when a child can see his parents growing in Christ and changing as God changes them. Real relationships are forged in the valleys (the vulnerable times of life). Mom's relationship with the Lord grew more intimate through this whole ordeal. Mom and I were able to grow closer together through the vulnerability of the illness.

I love you, David

Ann's perspective

I was not particularly excited to be with Mom on this ladies' retreat. I was still reeling from the effects of a "family discussion" we'd had the previous month and I really wanted to steer clear of my folks for a while. However, I was there and decided to make the best of it. I know now that it was in God's plan and design that I was with Mom to take care of her and to learn what God had to teach me about my relationship with my folks.

We'd had a good time the Friday night of the retreat, with no sign of the events soon to follow. Saturday morning we enjoyed a nice relaxed breakfast before heading to our meeting room. Mom was a little nervous, which is normal before she speaks. As she stood to speak, she got a funny look on her face and said, "Something up here is dead." I thought she meant the microphone until she turned white and scared-looking. When she said it again, I knew there was a problem and I rushed to her. I didn't have a clue what to do. I don't think I'd ever seen Mom helpless before. That's not exactly true though, because as she began to feel a little better, she thought going to the hospital was ridiculous. When we insisted, she just gave instructions all the way out the door for when she got back!

It scared her enough, however, that she did go. How thankful I am for that. God showed His providence in that we were just three or four minutes from the hospital and I was quite familiar with the emergency room procedure. (With four small children, I'd been there on more than one occasion!)

I was much relieved to turn Mom over to the ER personnel and had the confidence that they would know what to do. I never entertained the thought that she wouldn't be anything but okay. After all, I think we always believe that our parents are invincible. I did ... until this episode. And God used it to teach me a valuable lesson— my parents won't always be around, so I'd better appreciate them and learn all I can from them while I can. That may sound simple, but I'd never even considered the death of my folks. It showed me how insignificant the hurt feelings were that I'd been carrying around in light of the alternative. I praise God that Mom is fine and leaving a legacy for me and my children in the books she's written. I'm thankful, too, that God showed me *never* to take wonderful parents for granted!

Lan's perspective

The phone rang on that Saturday morning. We didn't get all that many calls from church members about trivial things, being in a middle-class city church. Lisa, Roland's wife, was on the other end with news that I wasn't going to like. She said Dad had called from his car on the way to Baton Rouge. Mom had been there doing a women's retreat for Barry and Ginny Foster's church. Ann was there with her when she felt her arm going numb. When sitting down and all the customary, cautionary measures didn't seem to help, a doctor who happened to be in the hotel recommended that they go to the hospital. That was it. Lisa was letting us all know for Dad, and someone would call as soon as he found what was going on.

Now I was the one who was numb. I knew life brought unexpected blind-sides, but I had been nailed. Everything had been going great: the Lord had moved me and my family 1,550 miles, from the swamp to the desert, to a high-tech mission field in Phoenix, Arizona, and we were as happy and as peaceful at being in the center of the will of God as we could be. We were a *long way* from family, but both sets of parents had been to see us (more of a challenge for mine than hers), a new child, new house, new church, new friends; God had been unloading boatloads of blessings on us. Life was good.

Then the phone call came. I sat in the kitchen for a while, trying to collect myself and my thoughts. After all, I always preached that stuff about God, Him meeting needs, being there for and with us in times of crisis and uncertainty, etc., etc. I didn't want to start dictating to God, but I think He was well aware that I wasn't ready to let go of our baby's namesake so soon. Susanne came in and when she saw me, teary and somewhat pale, she asked me what was wrong. We cried and held each other and prayed.

I sat there thinking, "Now what am I supposed to do?" The distance hadn't mattered until now. We were always talking to each other on the phone. The whole family was getting together in New Orleans the next month. Mom and Dad sent everyone a monthly itinerary, and this wasn't on it! The 1,550 miles might as well have been Mars. I felt so powerless, so limited. I was the one Mom always said was so good in a crisis. Here was a first-class crisis at full bore, and I couldn't do doodley-squat. What was *I* going to do now? What advice would I give to someone else? Was it good enough for me? Which direction would I take now that my back was against the wall?

Sometime right after Creation and before microwaves, God created the telephone! Susanne says I pick one up as soon as I wake up, walk in, or get within cellular range coming back into town. All I knew to do was to get some help ASAP. Looking back, I had Mom literally surrounded in prayer. She couldn't have gotten away if she had tried. I called Aunt Margaret in Newnan, Georgia. I called Dr. George Ritchie in Wichita Falls, Texas. I called Mom's best friend, Era Chastain, in Gulfport, Mississippi. I called the McDonalds in New Iberia, Michael Wethey in Baton Rouge, and Alvin Handley in Avondale. I even called my in-laws in Mobile. (You'll do lots of things when your back's against the wall!) With all of these friends and family members plugged in and getting prayer chains started, I figured I had done all I could do under the circumstances and with the limitations of time and space, while at the same time I had done the most important, most powerful thing I could do.

Later, when I did get to talk to Mom at the hospital in Baton Rouge, she asked me, "Did you have to call everybody?!" I didn't call everybody, but I did call those who mattered and the ones I knew we could count on in a crisis. The doctors had a lot of long names for what they found, but Mom's layman's translation was "bad brain waves!" That, in itself, was somewhat of a letdown, because as we all told her, "Heck, Mom, we've known that for years. We could have told you that!"

The Lord was Himself—faithful through it all. The fact that we were all planning to get together as a family anyway less than a month later proved to be providential. Susanne had told me if I felt like I needed to go, to go. There was nothing I could have done at the time and with a trip coming up, we decided to just wait and burn up the phone lines.

The whole episode was sort of the beginning of the refocusing of a lot of things for me. As the old adage goes, "The only thing permanent is *change.*" Although the deep feelings for and priority of family have always been extremely real and big with me, I was reminded again of the treasure of the days when we are together as well as the fact that one of these days, that'll change. Our family has been indescribably blessed in so many ways. Though separated now across several states, with the mobility Mom and Dad have and the various ministry and denominational opportunities we all have, we are able to get together more than most families. It does take planning, work, and flexibility, and very generous parents don't hurt the process one bit!

The importance of establishing new family traditions for the next generation becomes a matter of priority and practice. Living each day to the fullest and never falling to the temptation of taking any of our blessings for granted is a daily challenge as well as a Christian privilege. The money spent via US West and AT&T will one day prove to have been the best investment we could have ever made, both for us and our children. They will know their roots of family and faith.

Mom's episode brought changes for all of us, and many of them have been for our mutual benefit. Greater appreciation for family and time together is a big one. A tough one, possibly toughest for Mom, has been a greater understanding of the mysteries of God and His will for us. The world view, like Job's wife and friends had, looks for some negative or punitive reason for the difficulties of life. Mom struggled with this, big time. I can also see, from the outside looking in, that she has grown spiritually, maybe to a degree against her will, in ways that would have never happened without her episode. Had she never had this mortality check, we all know she wouldn't have changed some aspects of her life-style and scheduling. Although she has only taken baby steps in these areas, I really think she'd have continued at 90 mph and possibly taken years off her life, robbed herself and countless others of lessons from our Lord, and missed the depth of relationships with God, her husband, and her family that she has today.

The good news is that God is not through with her or the rest of us! Change is seldom our idea, and it definitely wasn't Mom's. I wouldn't have blueprinted things this way, but I'm not the Architect. . . . I cried out to God when I saw and heard her struggling for reasons and answers, torn apart by medicinal attempts to regulate her condition, and absolutely frustrated by the inability of the medical community to properly diagnose her problems for so long. The other side of this coin is faith. I'm not surprised, but through it all, for Mom and the rest of us, God has been Who He has always been and will continue to be, faithful. I just need those ongoing reminders that He isn't on my time schedule.

I have learned from her experience and my own the truth of the songwriter, "You can't stand up all by yourself, you can't stand up alone. You need the touch of a mighty hand, you can't stand up alone." I can't adequately express everything that I have learned or what God has done, but He has been working and is working, and He isn't through with her or me yet. . . .

Tangible Love

Our families are meant to offer hope, encouragement, and healing, and mine did just that. I never realized how independent I had come across to my children, but I came to realize anew how much I needed them and how much they needed me. When a family gathers around one as mine did me, once restored, you treasure those relationships even more.

JOURNAL ENTRY

We thank Thee, Our Father, for family. Help us to appreciate them and love them as we will wish we had done if we lost them.

Three things stand out in my family's support of me: *time, talk, touch.*

1) *Time.* Angel Martinez spells love *T-I-M-E,* and I do, too. A friend wrote me during this experience, "Time, prayer and patience are great healers—family and friends help it to happen. I know you will be fine. Only trust Him!"

Time is *everything* to a relationship. You can express respect and love for your loved ones by your *presence.* Loneliness kills like an invisible bullet. My main desire, and I feel that of others in pain, is to be in contact with those who care.

In our family we work at being together. This was true before my illness, and even more true now, I think. It takes advance planning and scheduling, compromise on dates and places, willingness to save and spend money, but mainly a basic "want to." According to Deut. 11:18-19, *every* family function can and should be sacred.

2) *Talk.* There is therapy in honest sharing. It seems almost anything, negative or positive, can be fixed by spending quality time together. My children were transmitters of warmth and love during this time, which brought caring, support, and comfort. I might add that the best response you can give hurting persons is to listen in a nonjudgmental way and try to understand why they feel the way they do. Every wounded person has a story punctuated with pain, and needs us to listen with sensitivity and compassion.

One counselor says, "People get so panicky about not knowing what to do or say that they shut the suffering person out to make themselves feel more comfortable." Sometimes we may avoid the suffering one rather than risk saying the wrong thing. It is amazing what healing words can do. Unfortunately, in our society there is little tolerance for another's sickness or pain. Too often we put sick people out of sight, or at least out of mind. Don't deny or minimize the problem and refrain from giving advice. The better thing is to acknowledge the difficult situation and let them talk about the problem, which may allow the healing process to begin. If they are slow to open up, *be patient.* They will begin to share when they are emotionally ready.

3) *Touch.* Bill Hybels says, "Despite all the miracle drugs nowadays, the best medicine for many ailments still is a *big hug* from somebody who cares." In fact, relationship itself begins with *"touch."* Physical touch is very important to someone who is hurting. Most simply need a shoulder to cry on. Touches say many words—and what a *joy* it is to receive an arm around your shoulder

or a warm embrace on days of discouragement. Positive reinforcement came to me when my family dared to reach out and touch me.

My David, my 6'5" 250-plus-pound youngest son, was a past master in administering a comforting hug during those low days. When he put those big arms around me and *squeezed,* it communicated *volumes.* There is no substitute for touch in the healing process.

Providing comfort takes forethought and sensitivity. We are all self-centered (Phil. 1:21), so developing an interest in the welfare of others is a cultivated skill. However, any friend or loved one can dispense the loving prescriptions of *time, talk,* and *touch.* Ask God to love through you the people who are most important in your life.

Dave and Jan Dravecky summed it up best when they wrote:

> The family, for all its flaws is God's most basic form of community. It's not a perfect community—neither is the church—but it is where we learn to care for one another. That's what families are for, to be there when you need them, to fix you chicken soup, to put fresh sheets on your bed, to get you through whatever it is you need help getting through.

PRAYER

Lord, thank You that crises can deepen rather than diminish our love for each family member. Give us an increased gratitude for our homes, which provide a foundation when the winds of life beat against the houses of our souls.

Questions for Chapter 6

1) What does your family mean to you? Reflect on the many ways they bless your life.

2) How has your family helped you during your times of crisis?

3) Show your family what they mean to you. Set some specific goals in each of these areas as you encourage your loved ones.

Time—

Talk—

Touch—

CHAPTER 7

Romance in the Journey

A GOOD MARRIAGE is not so much having the right partner as being the right partner. I want you to renew your vision about your marriage and your home. Think in terms of mending your marriage and marking your children. The greatest thing we can do to mark our children is to mend our marriages. Let's get busy at that task.

Most of us put on a good show. I can make you think everything is wonderful at home. I can make you think my family is ideal. Anybody knows that is not true. I have my problems just as you do. The outside of a package does not necessarily reveal the inside. We *all* have problem areas. Our marriages constantly need reassessment. There is nothing in this world worth enough to create a tear in our relationships.

One problem is that we have equated the wedding with marriage. That is as ridiculous as equating salvation and sanctification. They are not the same. Sanctification is the process toward maturity that follows the new birth. The wedding just marks the beginning of the journey called marriage that we work at for a lifetime.

Dr. David Mace, a noted Christian counselor, says most marriages operate at 90 percent of their level of potential. Any marriage, the best marriage, is not living up to its potential. Our priorities need constant readjustment. They so easily get out of whack. What about your home? Do you place it in the responsible position it ought to have in your life?

Recently, I have been studying a lesson series from the Revelation. For the first time, I began to understand what I had always felt were impossible passages to comprehend. I know that what John wrote to those seven churches had to do with our salvation relationship. However, as I sat and pondered those Scriptures, I began to apply them to my marriage. You can tell where my mind is. I am a homemaker to the core. My thoughts automatically moved to make the application in my home.

When John was speaking in Rev. 2:4 to the church in Ephesus he said, "Nevertheless, I have somewhat against thee, because thou hast left thy first love." We are constantly drawn outside the home in our "marriage-on-the-go" world. Men are busy; women are trying to prove themselves and their abilities; children are coming home to empty houses, earning the title "latch-key generation."

Why do you and I insist on giving ourselves to people who don't love us, at the expense of those who do? It is so easy to neglect our spouses, but notice John didn't say they lost their love, they just "left" it! You haven't lost the love you have one for the other as marriage partners, but you may have left it in the pursuit of "the good life." Then John gives timely advice in verse 5, "Remember, therefore, from whence thou art fallen, and repent, and do the first works." As my husband would say, "That will preach!" The emphasis is on the words *remember, repent,* and "do," or *revitalize* if you want an alliteration.

Remember How It Was

What are you going to remember? You are going to remember how it used to be. I can go back forty years in my mind's eye and see how good Landrum Leavell looked in that tuxedo at our wedding. He was the best-looking thing I had ever seen and, I might add, still is! I can remember how my heart beat and my palms sweated. I remember those telephone conversations when we would talk for a solid hour. Following the ceremony, married couples are pushed to think of anything to say. Remember those first days: how you felt and how good it was. Go back and *do* some of those first things.

Often boredom creeps into our marriages just as it creeps into our faith. The fire needs to be rekindled in our faith and family.

Have you ever wished you were married to another? You will come across someone who is so thoughtful of his wife, and you think, "I wish my husband was like that." Or you see someone who is so polite, and courteous, and you think, "My husband never does that. He never pulls a chair out for me." We think the grass might be greener on the other side of the fence. Somebody said, "If you ever think the grass is greener on the other side of the fence, just remember it has to be mowed, too!" You would just have to adjust to a whole new set of faults! When I question Landrum about the possibility of him remarrying he always says, "I wouldn't break in another wife for all the cows in Texas!"

I like the title of the book *The Care and Feeding of a Happy Marriage.* That lets us know marriage is something we must maintain. All marriages need attention. One preacher said, "We would not let our marriage work, we would *make* it work." Another said, "Couples are not automatically compatible; you *learn* to be compatible." Celebrate your differences. As Bill Hybels says, "Discover the complementary nature of frustrating differences!" A happy marriage is not a given. You have to *work* at meshing your differences, but it is well worth the effort.

There is no marriage that can't succeed, and there is no marriage that can't fail. There is no safe stage. What about your marriage? Is it in a rut? Is it boring or are you satisfied and fulfilled?

What did you do when you were courting? *Do it again!* We must rediscover romance and duplicate some of the circumstances we used to enjoy. I always loved, and I thought he loved, going to the movies when we were dating. We went every time the show changed. Granted, we are not old enough for most movies now! Nor do we have the time or the free nights to give to them, but I still enjoy a movie treat. There is nothing more romantic than to go to a movie, hold hands, and eat popcorn. That is as good as it gets!

A couple of years ago Landrum was in Nashville at a meeting. He says the only thing about his job he doesn't like is those meetings at the "Vatican"! However, he always checks in with me at night by phone, and tells me about his day. I remember the particular telephone conversation when he said, ". . . and I went to the show tonight." I said, "You what?" He said, "I went to the show tonight." I said, "You won't take me to the show, but you will go to Nashville and go to the show with Russell Dilday!" I could not believe it. I was *most* unhappy.

He saw *Driving Miss Daisy* so it was legitimate, but I was as mad as a hornet. He did redeem himself the other day, however. About six o'clock one evening he looked over at me and said, "Honey, do you have any plans for supper?" I said, "I will get up and fix it in a minute." Then he said, "Have you ever had any fried green tomatoes?" I said, "No, I have heard of them, but I have never eaten any." He said, "If you will hurry up and fix supper I will take you to see it." I squealed. I could not believe it. This guy was actually offering to take me to the movies. He was doing penance, I think. Anyway, we went to the movies and had the best time. Duplicating some of the circumstances of our courtship usually stirs up the fires of romance often lacking in our fast-paced marriages.

We periodically go to Charlie's Steak House in New Orleans. It is one of the old restaurants we used to go to on very special occasions. Landrum still reminds me of the times when he used to take me and I could not eat a whole steak! That has been awhile, but if I am going to plan something that I know he will enjoy, we go to Charlie's—another carry-over from our courtship days.

Marge Caldwell suggests that we set aside a regular date night. It will never "just happen" in our busy lives unless we make it a priority. If you can't manage every week, make it once every two weeks or even once a month.

Her suggestion is that you plan it one week, and let him plan it the next. When I plan the date night, I am trying to think of what would appeal to Landrum. When he plans the date night, he is going to think of what would appeal to me. Do you see what that does to your marriage? It keeps you thinking about your partner and not yourself. That is the whole purpose. Think about it. If I am going to plan a date night for Landrum, where am I going to take him to eat? Charlie's. It is not as good as it used to be, and I keep telling him that, but that is still where he wants to go. If he is going to plan a date night for me, we are going to the movies or to Houston's, my favorite restaurant. *Remember* how it was, and once again rediscover the romance that perhaps has cooled with the passage of time. I promise you it won't be nearly as icy between those sheets!

Repent

John said to the church at Sardis, "Remember therefore how thou hast received and heard, and hold fast, and repent" (Rev. 3:2). *Repent.* Other translations say, "be watchful," or "wake up, and strengthen what remains." Men and women can use amazing creativity when it comes to their jobs, and can be the dumbest when it comes to building the home. If we used some of the same ingenuity in our homes, we would have happier spouses. The scriptural admonition is, get busy. Inner decay works when we are not busy revitalizing our relationships. If a couple continues to engage in the activities that brought them together, the marriage will be a good one.

Remember and repent of the fact that you have not spent enough time together. Return to the value and importance of the home. Couples abandon their relationships to build churches or fortunes, and they end up with fortunes, but at the expense of their homes. If you don't work at balancing family and career, I guarantee you, your life is going to tilt toward your work. One pastor who had lots of family problems said, "When your home crumbles, all of those super churches in the world lose their significance." You are not going to enjoy success in any realm if you forfeit your homelife. Someone said, "If you want to know if you are led by the Spirit of God, don't check your ministries, check your homelife. If it won't work there, don't export it."

Repent. Understand that love needs constant care and attention. Intimacy takes time. Nurturing a relationship and causing it to grow takes time. I think that Landrum and I love each other more today after forty years than we did after a year. It has had *time.* We've grown and ministered together. We have parented and played together. We have done all of those things that build a relationship "together." Intimacy seldom occurs "doing your own thing," as is the custom today.

Revitalize

When we first fell in love, it probably began in this order. First, there were those unexplained "feelings" of joy and delight in the presence of the other. Second, we "acted" on those feelings and arranged time together at every possible moment. Third, we made a "commitment" to one another for life.

It has been suggested that in order to get the "feelings" of early marriage back, we must reverse that process. We make a "commitment" to *remember* and *repent,* then we "act" on that commitment by purposely *revitalizing* our marriage, and the "feelings" will return. When we return to our first love, we can enjoy our first blessings.

This is a difficult assignment, and is the opposite of selfishness and apathy. However, it is exactly what Paul described in 1 Cor. 13 as the epitome of love. The neat thing about doing things God's way is that *it works.* Though the assignment is difficult, it is also dependable because "love never fails" (1 Cor. 13:8). We may fall out of lust, but *never* out of love! Lust is a feeling, but love is a choice—a commitment. The joy of a relationship depends foundationally on commitment, understanding that nothing is more important than family relationships and that they are the center of life and the source of life's deepest joys.

Get to work *revitalizing* your relationship. Recapture some of the excitement. Spend less time sticking to your routine. Try to break up your schedule. Landrum and I were talking the other day about our need to be more spontaneous. We get locked into routines doing the same old thing. We were driving recently from Daytona Beach, Florida to New Orleans. That is a long way and naturally we were anxious to get home after that length of time in the car. However, we stopped in Gulfport, Mississippi to see a friend in the hospital. We thoroughly enjoyed seeing him. While there, we found out another friend was in the same hospital so we went to see her and had a nice visit with both. I said, "Honey, I don't want us to get so locked into a routine that we never do anything spontaneously." That stop in Gulfport was not planned, but it ministered to us as well as to our friends.

We miss some wonderful things in life because we are such creatures of habit and often stick with what's familiar to us. Keep eyes and ears open to new experiences God might have for you. Diversify and change the way you do things, especially the small things. Stop at a roadside park. Stop on the side of the road at an antique shop just for fun. Do something exciting and different to break the routine. How long has it been since you have done something fresh, frivolous, and unplanned? Probably a long time. Revitalize your relationship. Put the words of this old song into practice: "I'm going to find me a new way to light up an old flame!" Be as creative there as you are in other areas of your life.

The complaint I get from wives is their relationships are boring.

Max Lucado wrote concerning familiarity and Satan's strategy:

> Nor will he steal your home from you; he'll do something far worse. He'll paint it with a familiar coat of drabness. He'll replace evening gowns with bathrobes, nights on the town with evenings in the recliner, and romance with routine. He'll scatter the dust of yesterday over the wedding pictures in the hallway until they become a memory of another couple in another time.
>
> He won't take your children; he'll just make you too busy to notice them. His whispers to procrastinate are seductive. There is always next summer to coach the team, next month to go to the lake, and next week to teach Johnny how to pray. He'll make you forget that the faces around your table will soon be at tables of their own. Hence, books will go unread, games will go unplayed, hearts will go unnurtured, and opportunities will go ignored. All because the poison of the ordinary has deadened your senses to the magic of the moment.
>
> Before you know it, the little face that brought tears to your eyes in the delivery room has become—perish the thought—common. A common kid sitting in the back seat of your van as you whiz down the fast lane of life. Unless something changes, unless someone wakes you up, that common kid will become a common stranger.

Reality

Fred Lowery, a preacher friend of ours, suggested an acrostic using the word "rut." The *R* is for *reality*. The reality is that *every* marriage is difficult and has dry spells. Landrum and I have gone through those in our relationship. When we sense we are in a dry spell, it is time to do something different.

There are no perfect marriages any more than there are perfect homes. You don't put two imperfect people together, from different backgrounds, and expect not to have problems. To a degree, we all come from dysfunctional families. I said that in my seminary class and one student took exception. She said, "I resented it when Mrs. Leavell said nobody had a perfect childhood. I grew up thinking I did." Well, more power to her. Believe me, in my experience, she is an exception. Few of us have had a perfect background.

The reality is that opposites usually attract. These differences bring excitement to marriage, but also conflict. Marriage is giving up "me" to be part of "us," and most of us don't give up "me" very easily. Our differences can become a deep source of conflict. Are you and your husband exactly alike? No!

I heard one counselor say that when couples come together at the marriage altar they dump their raw material much like supplies at a building site. He dumps his raw material and she dumps hers. Then they spend a lifetime putting this together.

My pile of raw material included my background, parents, sisters and brothers, education, self-esteem, and the way I celebrated holidays. His raw material included the same sorts of things. Then we spend a lifetime merging these in a wholesome way.

There could not have been two people with more differences than Landrum and me. He came from a loving Christian home. His mother and daddy loved him and prayed for him. He had two sisters and his father was a Baptist pastor. I came from a home where my folks were nominal Christians. They showed up on Sunday mornings and weren't fired up at all with my decision to marry a preacher. My daddy didn't even call his name for six months. He thought if he ignored him, he would go away. We had our differences. In fact, our oldest son looks at Landrum occasionally and says, "Dad, you know what? You really took a chance on Mom, didn't you?" He took a big chance because of our differing backgrounds.

I look at people all the time and wonder how in the world they ever got together. They appear to have nothing in common, and they probably don't. We *learn* to be compatible. We work through our problems and learn from our differences. The sad thing is that most church people don't like to admit they have any problems. The church is the easiest place on the face of the earth to "fake it." We put on our "everything is perfect" faces, and never admit even to ourselves that problems exist. The reality is that half of our marriages are coming apart. In our attempts to cover up any difficulties in our marriages, we don't even admit them to ourselves. Usually by the time we seek some help, it is too late.

My best advice is to seek help. If you have any sort of problem in your marriage, don't pretend. Don't sweep it under the rug, but get some help for any trouble spots you detect. Chuck Swindoll's book *Strike the Original Match* reminds us that the original match is usually best. True love does not die. The Bible says, "Love never fails." True love may lie dormant for a while, but it is there. It is up to us to rekindle the fire.

I want to introduce you to a super book, *His Needs, Her Needs,* by Willard Harley. The author talks about how to "affair proof" your marriage based on the Word of God. He is not a theologian but gives sound advice. He talks in that book about building a relationship with romance, increasing intimacy, and deepening our awareness of each other and our varying needs. He points to five needs of men and five needs of women.

Understanding

Understanding is the *U* in our "rut" acrostic. You must attempt to understand your mate. The problem in most marriages is that we are meeting needs that don't exist. We need to know the needs of our mates before we can meet them. Let me illustrate with two of my three sons. One is a hunter and the other an avid golfer. Wouldn't I be stupid to give my son who is crazy about hunting, golf clubs for Christmas? Or the golfer a gun? Why? Because that is not what they want or need. Yet that is exactly what we do in the marriage relationship. I am trying to meet needs of my husband based on how I want my needs met. He is trying to meet needs of mine based on how he wants his met, and it doesn't work. If we build a relationship that is going to sustain romance throughout the long haul, we must have an awareness of the other's needs.

According to Harley, a wife's needs are first of all for affection. That is nonsexual touching. Women have a strong need to be appreciated and loved. The second is for conversation. There are few women who don't complain, "My husband just doesn't talk to me." We like conversation. It is said, "A man loves with his eyes but a woman loves with her ears." She likes to hear those sweet nothings! The third is for honesty and openness. We want him to tell us his inmost thoughts. We want him to tell us how he feels and what he thinks. So often we have to *pull* that out of him. The fourth need is for financial support. We need security in that area. And the last is for commitment. We want him to be committed to the family, where we move together in an atmosphere of companionship and need.

His first need in marriage is sexual fulfillment. Whom does that surprise? The typical wife does not understand her husband's deep need for sex any more than a husband understands his wife's need for affection. We are different. We are not only physically plumbed differently, we are emotionally "wired" differently. Someone said, "Men are a microwave and women are a crockpot!"

If you don't try to understand your husband here, there will always be somebody around who will. That is not a threat of any kind, but it is true. Clandestine sexual fulfillment is never God's way of meeting our needs. Safe sex is God's plan from the start. However, we must not tempt him to sin. I am not saying there is any excuse for a man to sin, but I am saying we may be giving Satan a big advantage by our negligence at this point.

Prepare for lovemaking. What do we wear but old T-shirts and faded gowns? The last thing we spend a dime on is lingerie to please our husbands, and I am as guilty as you are.

I have a good friend who says her husband likes for her to have pretty nightgowns—the dainty, skimpy variety. Before going on a cruise for their twenty-fifth wedding anniversary, my friend bought some new nighties. After returning she went to lunch with a group of friends from her church. Following lunch they decided to shop for a while. As they made their way through one store, there was one of the nighties she had bought on a mannequin. About the time they walked by it, one in the group said, "Wonder who in the world would buy that?" My friend said, "I don't know. I just can't imagine!"

A loving encounter with our spouse can be a panacea for other ills, at least a temporary one. Our husbands are under tremendous stress. They are covered up with jobs, responsibilities, financial obligations, and many other demands. Isn't it wonderful that God has provided at least a temporary panacea for those problems?

On our campus recently we had a seminar for student wives and guess what the subject was? "Behind the Bedroom Door." Crumbling marriages are not just a problem in the world, but in the church, and among our ministry students. We are attempting to address this as we educate couples regarding their mates' needs.

The second need of a man is for recreational companionship.

This is second in importance only to sex. According to Harley, before marriage we spend fifteen hours a week in this way. What happens after marriage? We do very little, if anything, together. We are so busy; therefore, we go our way and he goes his. Often we are like two ships who pass in the night. This is not enough to maintain a romantic relationship over the long haul, and never forget that romance paves the road of love on our marriage journey. His need for a recreational companion is real and Scripture says in Col. 3:18, "Wives adapt yourselves to your husbands, that your marriage may be a Christian unity" (Phillips). Adapt yourself. Someone else has said, "Learn the wisdom of compromise for it is better to bend a little than to break." I heard it another way. "If you lean over backwards at least you are not going to fall on your face."

If you don't enjoy the things he enjoys, learn to like them. I had a sister who did that. Her husband was an avid hunter. He was a doctor, and when he wasn't practicing medicine, he was hunting. She finally decided that if she ever wanted to see him, she was going to have to go with him. She began to accompany him bird hunting and learned to love it. She could talk with as much enthusiasm as he could about that sport.

My sister-in-law married a jeweler. She knew absolutely nothing about the jewelry business but she learned. She became a bridal consultant, and worked right beside him. There are times when we must adapt and take on the life-styles of our husbands.

Harley's book lists about fifty activities. He suggests that the husband go down the list and check what he likes to do. The wife then checks what she likes to do. Somewhere in that list of fifty, you are bound to come up with something you can do together. I am not saying that every waking minute you need to do things together because that is impossible. You are going to have your areas of interest, and he is going to have his, but at some point you must come together and connect. Men are recreational beings. If we are to meet the needs of our husbands, being recreational companions is a must.

Landrum likes to hunt. I don't like to hunt. I shop. He doesn't like to shop. However, we do like to work together, talk together, and travel together. There are lots of things we enjoy together. If you want your marriage to stay fresh, find something in the recreational area that you can do together. Experiment. Make yourself find a mutual interest and I guarantee it will benefit your marriage.

The third need a man has is for an attractive spouse. Men are visual beings. Remember? "A man loves with his eyes." Pride enters into this because when you look good, it makes him look good. If you look like an old hag, he is diminished in the eyes of his peers.

I always tell my student wives to look for things they *can* control to improve their appearance. We can do very little about inherited physical characteristics, but we can be neat, clean, stylish, and constantly seek to highlight our *best* features.

A man has a need for a wife who cares about her personal appearance. I often hear this verse quoted by those who take little pride in their appearance. ". . . For man looketh on the outward appearance, but the Lord looketh on the heart" (1 Sam. 16:7). The fact is, your husband is not God! He looks on the outward appearance, and it is important that he likes what he sees or this becomes another area that is a prime target for the enemies of Christ.

The fourth need is for domestic support. Prov. 17:1 says, "Better a dry crust with peace and quiet than a house full of feasting with strife" (NIV®). We do not want to live in a little hell on earth. Titus essentially says that we are to manage our households well to ensure that God's message should not fall into disrepute (Titus 2:4, 5). When a husband can come home to a house that is quiet, well maintained, and cared for, it reduces his stress level unbelievably.

I am not saying that you have to do everything. Compromise on a fair division of labor. Especially if you work outside the home, you must agree on the things you are responsible for, and the things he is responsible for. Enlist help from your children.

The last need is for admiration. Eph. 5:33 says: "Let the wife see that she respects and reverences her husband. That she notices him, regards him, honors him, prefers him, esteems him, and that she defers to him, praises him, and loves and admires him exceedingly" (Amplified Bible).

What a wonderful translation of that verse. It tells us exactly what we are to do. We are to admire and notice him. He has a need for that attention. Don't let him get all his strokes from others. His work takes him into the marketplace where he is going to get all kinds of attention and admiration from others. You know and I know that it means much more coming from family. It means ten times more to me if Landrum says, "Honey, you did a good job."

Or if one of my children says, "Mom, you did good," it means more than for a thousand other people to say the same thing. Don't neglect his need for admiration.

We probably admire 90 to 95 percent of things about our husbands. However, we dwell on the 5 to 10 percent we don't like. We pick and pick and have the tendency to "major" on minors. I learned something last fall from my study in Philippians. In Phil. 1:3 Paul says, "I thank my God upon every remembrance of you." I wanted to say, "Paul, get real. I have been in ministry long enough to know that you did not like everybody in Philippi." Even though that was one of his most harmonious churches, I know that everybody in Philippi did not like him either. Yet Paul says, "I thank my God upon every remembrance of you." How could I explain that? I will tell you. Paul was thinking about the *total picture*. He was not willing to allow specks to spoil the whole. To me that is a lesson for our marriages, and for all areas of our lives. We can dwell on the specks or we can begin to accentuate the positive. Alex Haley suggests, "Find the good and praise it." Wouldn't it change the atmosphere in most homes if we simply said, "I thank my God upon every remembrance of you"?

Talk

The *T* in "rut" is for *talk*. Most men are logical and analytical beings. A man speaks about twelve thousand words a day. A woman speaks about twenty-five to thirty thousand a day. Do you see the problem? When a man gets home he has used up his twelve thousand, but most women have several thousand to go! We want him to talk. He wants to be quiet. This is why women need friends. We must have someone to unload those other words on! Communication is the key to a great marriage. When we listen to each other with undivided attention we are saying, "You are important enough for me to listen to you." Time to talk and listen is a big order in our busy world, but it is one that will pay rich dividends. Talk! Listen!

Our problem goes back to our constant activity. We live in an age of instant dinners, instant success, and instant intimacy, which by the way is a contradiction in terms. In our busy lives we don't have time for long, drawn-out conversation. No wonder there is so little real intimacy in marriage. Becoming best friends with your spouse takes time. And most of us do not have that time unless we make this cultivation a major priority.

The Lord gave us the pattern as He devoted time to spend with those closest to Him. We find Him walking with Enoch and Noah, talking with Moses, eating with Abraham, and think of the long afternoons He spent with Mary, Martha, and Lazarus. He relished conversation with these various personalities because His priority was people.

Ask yourself some of these questions. Are we close? Do we communicate well? Are we in touch with each other's lives? I hope you can answer all of these questions in the affirmative. I hope you can say yes, we are in touch. Yes, we communicate. Yes, we are close. I hope you have a wonderful relationship. If you do, chances are you remember, have repented, and are constantly revitalizing your relationship. Keep up the good work!

Love is a decision, not a feeling. We can love until the feeling comes back. If your marriage is dormant right now, stir up the coals. I guarantee you the blaze will return. Begin to do some of the things you did that made you fall in love in the first place. We are usually our own worst enemy. We create many of our own problems by choosing not to be happy. Someone said, "If I kicked the one most responsible for my problems, I could not sit down for a week!" Only the grace of God plus commitment make it possible to have a happy marriage in the world in which we live. Marriage is daily, but it does not have to be dull. If your marriage is dull, then go to work to bring back the romance.

Prov. 12:4 describes two kinds of marriages. The first is, "A virtuous woman is a crown to her husband." The second "is as rottenness in his bones." Which one is yours?

PRAYER

"Lord, I will try to walk a blameless path, but how I need Your help, especially in my own home, where I *long* to act as I should" (Ps. 100:2 TLB).

Questions for Chapter 7

1) If you are married, what kind of marriage partner are you? If you are not married, what kind of marriage partner would you desire to be? Write your answer below.

2) Read Rev. 2:4-5. Apply John's truths to your marriage. Set some goals to *remember, repent,* and *revitalize* your marriage relationship.

3) How are you using your personality differences to make "us" stronger in your marriage?

CHAPTER 8

Journey with Friends

THERE IS A FOURTH CERTAINTY that possesses me: I am certain that my life would not be as rich and full had it not been for my deep and lasting friendships. Friends are absolutely indispensable. Some people in ministry say you can't have them. I say you won't make it without them! Landrum and I have been *so* blessed with those who have stood by us through the years. I think you miss one of life's great joys if you don't have deep friendships.

When the hard times come, God loves us through the real arms of His children. Your friends can love and sustain you as you move through "your" valley. I can testify to the truth that God always provides some person who knows and understands, listens, and loves. We are truly the Lord's gifts to one another in the crises of life. As I look back, I see that encouragement came to me from many of my friends. It may have been a call, a card, or a Scripture included in a handwritten note. Maybe it was a book sent.

A lady in my son's church in Phoenix sent me a devotional book I have treasured. I have read and reread it. I just ordered six to give to people who are hurting. I seldom do anything halfway! It is an old classic, *Streams in the Desert*. Many of you have read it. Perhaps it would not have meant as much had I not been in the desert, but every page spoke to me. The gift card said, "I just felt impressed to send you this." Who impressed her? God's Spirit. Anita Bryant says, "He guides us at times with almost imperceptible inner nudges which often lead us to certain people." The Holy Spirit impressed her.

I have asked myself, "Jo Ann, how many times has the Lord impressed you and you failed to act?" How many times has He spoken to me and I was just too busy to listen? Someone may need your note, the book you would send, a visit, flowers, food, prayers, or just the right Scripture. Be God's answer to someone's prayer. I have learned that you never forget those who ministered to you in a time of need.

God's surprises often come from people in strange wrappings. Don't discount anybody. That unlikely person may be the one who ministers to you best. Although this experience has been painful, I also gained a great deal. I gained not only a deeper appreciation for those relationships I once took for granted, but also a closer, more loving concern for my fellow human beings. When my own faith faltered I hung on to theirs!

Do you remember the paralytic described in Mark 2:1-12 whose four friends brought him to Jesus? They let him down through the roof because of the crowd, and Jesus saw "their" faith. Christianity is not a solo sport. Sometimes we have to borrow faith and encouragement from others when we are weak.

It is extremely important to pray with grieving people, but we may need to do the praying for them. In the early stages of grief or illness, most people are numb and unable to verbalize their prayers so we have to communicate with God for them.

One of our trustees ministered to me in prayer. At the time, I was not seeing anybody, yet he asked if he could just come pray for me. He did, and I will long remember his concern voiced in prayer for me and my well-being. It was one of those truly healing moments.

We need those friends who are willing to share our tears, carrying and praying us through the valleys. Timothy said about Onesiphorus, "He often refreshed me." I'm so glad there are those who know how to touch a life and can enter into someone's pain and hurt with understanding, tact, and tenderness.

Life has its ups and downs, but joy can come in the downs as well as the ups if we learn the value of our faith, the importance of our family, and the treasure of our friends. We need the stimulation from a variety of relationships. Don't miss these blessings for they bring joy.

When you are away from close family ties, you will need the blessing of good friends for survival. The next best thing to family is good friends. There are a lot of people, especially in ministry, who think this spawns jealousy and division among your members. I'll have to say that my experience has been positive at this point.

Often we have a lot of acquaintances, but there is something special about good, close friends. Acquaintances are there for the good times, but friends get past the shallow waters of small talk and know the real "me." Do you have a close friend? I mean a genuinely close friend you can trust and with whom you can be transparent. If not, ask God to give you a close friend, one you can talk to, confide in, and depend on you when you need help and strength.

Replenishment

I was intrigued by Bill and Lynne Hybels' discussion of three types of relationships in their book, *Fit to Be Tied*. First, there are *draining* relationships, the kind that sap your energy. These are people you may not have anything against, but you don't feel comfortable around them and you have little in common. These are usually "takers" in the relationship and not "givers." A friend is to value—not to impose.

Next, there are *neutral* relationships. These are okay, but you are not highly motivated to maintain them because they don't enhance your life in any way.

Finally, there are *replenishing* relationships, which bring much joy to life. Replenishers are those who love you as you are and allow you to relax and talk freely. You don't have to weigh every word because there is no hidden agenda. These friends are just fun to be around. When you leave, everybody feels refreshed.

Hybels pointed out that Jesus intentionally exposed Himself to draining relationships as He taught and healed. People in helping professions are constantly exposed to those who take from them and give nothing back, which is the very essence of Christian ministry.

Jesus also had neutral relationships with friends and disciples, but remember how often He went to those "replenishers" in His life. Peter, James, and John have often been referred to as the "inner circle." The home of Mary, Martha, and Lazarus was a frequent stopping place for rest and refreshment. If Jesus needed replenishers in His life, how much more do we? Those are "soul mates" who breathe life into us and provide real joy in the journey.

The home of my sister-in-law, Margaret, has always been a "replenishing" place for me. I knew if I ever got to her home, I would be accepted, loved, nourished, and refreshed. What more could one ask? That must have been the way Jesus felt about the home of Mary, Martha, and Lazarus. I believe that, at least in part, explains his frequent visits there.

My friend Era's home has been another such place through the years. I was even welcomed there with four little children! There were not many places back in those days about which that could be said. So if I didn't love Era for any other reason, I would love her for making me feel welcome at a time in my life when I needed acceptance and friendship. As much as anyone ever has, Era makes me feel comfortable being myself. I never have to be "on" with her, or put on a good impression. We enjoy each other's company, we like the same things, and no matter how busy I am, I'm never too busy for a visit with this "replenisher" in my life. Many other homes could be added to this list, and I'll always be grateful the Lord gave me numerous "replenishing" stations along the way that have added much joy in my journey.

Landrum joins me in heartfelt gratitude for these and others who have lightened our load. We both have the strong desire for our home to be a "way station" for weary travelers who have our same need for encouragement and love. We talk frequently about the "replenishers" in our lives who have built us up and propped us up when we have been emotionally depleted.

One church friend proved to be a real "prop-er-upper" for me. He was in the group skiing with us in New Mexico one year during the Christmas holidays. After our move to New Orleans we were having withdrawal from our friends, so we met many of them for a winter vacation.

On a trip like that I am at my best drinking hot chocolate in the lodge! This was due at least in part to the fact that renting skis for our four children was about all we could afford. However, when they came in for a break, Landrum and I would borrow their equipment and "play" a little on the baby slopes.

This particular day I had watched the skiers come down the small slope in front of the lodge window with great interest. They appeared to be having such fun that I decided to ride the lift up and try it myself—which I did. The only problem was, that "small" slope from the top looked exactly like Mount Everest! I literally *froze.*

After quickly assessing the situation, I sat down in the snow to relieve myself of my skis. I put one under one arm and one under the other, and started sidestepping down "Mount Everest." I had just begun my trek down the mountain when a friend from our church appeared out of nowhere. In full control he said, "Jo Ann, sit down and put your skis back on." I guess since I was acting like a child he determined the best approach was to treat me like one. In my childlikeness, I put my skis back on. Then he said, "I'm going to ski right alongside of you and I'll get you down."

There is no way to describe the relief I felt when one came along to prop me up on my "leaning" side. These many years later I can still remember my fright that day and my gratitude for this encouragement and help.

One lady took it upon herself to "raise" a twenty-two-year-old preacher's wife. She taught me to cook and fed us many a meal. Another couple old enough to be our parents took us under their wing, and helped us over many rough spots in our hardest pastorate.

I still need "replenishers," and I feel that one of the greatest ways God can use a Christian is as a replenisher in the life of another. My life has certainly been enriched in my ministry to the student wives at New Orleans Seminary. I recently had the privilege of outfitting one of these young mothers who had just miscarried with twins. She admitted she needed a "lift," and to see the sparkle return was well worth any effort or time on my part.

In fact, my life was literally changed several years ago with a single phone call from a longtime friend. I remember it well because it was right before Easter when my friend called and said, "Jo Ann, do you know a student wife at the Seminary who might need a new Easter outfit?" I said quickly, "Not right this minute, but I'll bet I can find one!"

It didn't take me long, and this began my "shopping ministry" with student wives. Some years later my friend called at Christmas with the same request, and one year it was even Thanksgiving. I was curious as to why Thanksgiving this particular year, so I asked. The reply was, "Because I may not be here Christmas." I can't think of a better reason to be diligent about our acts of encouragement.

Well, my friend continued supporting my shopping-ministry "habit" for years until his health deteriorated. But by that time, I was *hooked!* I have continued this ministry and have tried to pick those who for one reason or another needed a "boost." To keep from being partial in any way, I have gotten assistance from our Dean of Students, who is more in contact with the "real" needs of those on campus than perhaps anyone else.

The first recipient was the mother of a child with spina bifida who was going through a real financial crunch. The neat thing is not only what this action does for the wives' wardrobes but for them as individuals. I have seen shy, retiring students literally come "alive" and blossom. One said to me, "Oh, Mrs. Leavell, I feel just like Cinderella!"

When I finished outfitting this particular Cinderella, I looked down at the loafers she was wearing and asked, "Now, honey, you *do* have shoes to go with these clothes, don't you?" I'll never forget the look on her face when she said, "No, ma'am, these are the only shoes I have." Needless to say, our next stop was the shoe store.

When my friend suggested the first outfit, he said, "Now, Jo Ann, I want to buy them a *nice* dress." With the capable assistance of another good friend of mine who is connected with a moderately priced store, we have literally translated that "nice" dress into five or six separates that can be interchanged to make several outfits. On the most recent shopping spree, the young girl said to me, "Oh, Mrs. Leavell, I have never had this many new clothes!" With her permission and that of her husband, we included an updated haircut just in time to have her picture made for her church's pictorial directory. Needless to say, she was elated!

My experience has been that we never give out more than the Lord gives back. He has blessed me in more ways than I can number from this ministry. Not only have the wives been appreciative, but I had one letter from a husband telling me what a difference this had made in the life of his wife.

For years I felt that gratitude was a thing of the past, but I have found it to be alive and well. The greatest indication came from Cinderella, who was very insistent in her plea to do something for my generous friend. She even mentioned baking him a cake until I told her he lived in another city. I assured her I would pass on to him her desire to reciprocate, but I told her that one day she would be in a position to help another.

The very next year at Christmastime, Cinderella stopped me in the hall. She said, "Mrs. Leavell, are you going to outfit a student wife this year?" I assured her that I was, and then she handed me an envelope and said, "I want to buy the shoes!"

My prayer is that you will find a need and meet it, and if you have been on the other end of someone else's generosity that you will determine to "buy the shoes" for another. Replenishers are always needed in our wounded society.

Usually when we Leavells get together as a family, we try on the last night to get the grandchildren to bed and have some "adult" talk. We share things going on in our lives. We share prayer requests and how we can minister to each other. The last time we did this, my daughter-in-law who had just moved to Phoenix, Arizona, said, "I need a friend. I need for you to pray the Lord will send me a close friend."

Being so far away from family, she did need a friend. For months we prayed for Susanne to find a friend and do you know where she found her? Catty-cornered across the street! It never ceases to amaze me how the Lord works. This friend is a Christian—not Baptist, but Lutheran. They like the same things, enjoy walking together, and crafts. Now they are in a Bible study together. The Lord can meet our needs for friends and for friendship.

My special friend, Era, sent me a card about every other day during my illness. Most had notes on them. She would say, "Jo Ann, when I hurt, Psalm so-and-so speaks to me. Read it." I would read it and it would speak to me, too. I will never forget those who walked with me through my wilderness experience.

God never wastes anything. I don't care what you are going through, it is not going to be wasted. You are going to be able to share those experiences with somebody. If you are hurting right now, you are going to meet somebody down the road and be able to say, "I know exactly how you feel." For heaven's sake, don't say that unless you have been down that same road! I cannot say to people, "I know how you feel going through a divorce," because I have never been there. I can't say, "I know how you feel," if you are widowed, because I have not lost my husband. I have never lost a child. I have never miscarried. I cannot tell those people that I understand. We have never been asked to leave a church. However, I have had an undiagnosed illness for a long time. I have been depressed, and know what it is like to be at "wit's end corner." I have had other instances in which I can say, "I know how you feel. When I hurt this is the verse that spoke to me." Your experience will mean something to those in a similar situation.

God's Friendship Pattern

Let's look at God's friendship pattern. I read about a decorator who, going out on a new job, said she always liked to question the people living in the home about their life-style, what they liked and disliked, in order to get a feel for the home. One question she usually asked was, "Do you have a special treasure you want me to see?" One such customer said, "I have three special treasures. My view, my music system, and my friends." Do you see your friends as special treasures? They are.

Men and women seem to be different in their need for friendship. I am told that only 10 percent of men have close friends whereas friends help women survive. Another woman can uniquely sympathize with female characteristics and needs.

I want to point out some of these differences I found extremely interesting. Boys are activity oriented whereas girls are people oriented. Boys prefer teams whereas girls like single best friends. Women have a stronger need for friendships and are three times more likely to have best friends. Men's friendships are less intimate. Men relate on the head level and there is very little give-and-take in a conversation with a man. Women relate on a heart level and appear to be free and intimate. Someone said, "In our society it seems you have to have a bosom to be a buddy."

Years ago, I'm told, Hallmark did an elaborate survey and developed a line of friendship cards for women. Hallmark was smart. If they had developed a line of friendship cards for men, they would have gone broke. Who buys the cards in your family? Who sends the birthday cards and buys the gifts? Usually it is women.

I am confident this is why the Lord gave us the ability to bear the children—we have this caring personality. Remember, however, there are exceptions to every rule. Many men relate like women, and there are lots of women who think like men. In general, however, boys grow up competing; girls grow up playing dolls. Masculinity is defined by separateness and femininity is defined by attachment. We are often the friendship makers in most families. I am glad I am a woman, and so glad God has given us the wonderful gift of friendship.

If we are going to have friends, one of the clearest truths of the New Testament is that love is active and not passive. Walter Winchell defines a friend as "one who walks in when others walk out." Adversity sifts friendship. Real friends are those who walk with you through those valley experiences.

If we are active in friendship, it means we are committed to helping each other. You see, I was no fun during my illness! Nobody would have wanted to be around me because of my scintillating company. In those days I could only receive, but my true friends were the ones who were willing to give.

Gal. 6:2 says, "Bear ye one another's burdens. . . ." I am told this refers to a "temporary" overload rather than an everyday one. We can't carry people for life. There are those emotional cripples who often try to attach themselves to us. There is no way we have the strength to carry needy people over the long haul. They need professional help. What I am talking about are those individuals who are experiencing temporary discomfort from sorrows, illness, or some other difficulties.

Do you know a hurting person? If so, assist him or her. Hurting people find it difficult to verbalize their need for help. They seldom know what they need. I could not have told you what I needed, but I am so glad that I had friends who stepped in and helped me.

I don't think I would have made it without my friend, Carol. She could have taught a course in Friendship 101! She often called to say, "Jo Ann, what are you going to do today?" I would say, "I have a doctor's appointment at 10:00." Her reply was often, "Why don't you let me take you?" My pride would never have allowed me to ask her, but she knew what I needed when I didn't. She took me, picked me up, and usually insisted on a cup of coffee on the way home. It was such a help.

How long do you assist? As long as necessary. Healing is so different for each one of us. It may take a longer time for some than others, but that is the price of friendship. We stay "alongside." When we encourage others, we get as close to doing the work of the Holy

Spirit as we can get. The Holy Spirit is "One called alongside." He is the One who lives in us, walks with us, talks with us, and strengthens us.

Admit it when you need that sort of help. So much of the time our pride will not let us be vulnerable, but I think you will find your vulnerability will draw people to you. When others know we have problems, they are more prone to open up and share their needs. I am not saying to air all your dirty linen. I am just saying, be transparent to the degree that makes you feel comfortable. When you admit problems, you open the way for people to tell you things. You open the door for them to say, "I have that same problem; how do you handle it?" You can point them to the Lord and the Word of God.

I don't know if you have read any of Alexandra Stoddard's books or not. They are good but her life is too "perfect". I can't relate to perfection. If I took her books literally, I would have to have at least forty-eight hours in every day to accomplish everything she suggests. I can't deal with that, and I think we turn people off by not admitting our vulnerability.

You remember the story of Ruth and Naomi. Scripture says in Ruth 3:16 that when Ruth came in from being with Boaz "she told Naomi everything." The *King James Version* says, "She told it all." Isn't that just like a woman? We are much quicker to tell all than men. Men are usually more hesitant to admit a problem than we are. Maybe that is just another facet of the man's ego. Men are good at finding solutions, but women provide comfort. Men are better at giving advice. However, if we are hurting we don't need advice. We just need somebody to hold us and comfort us. Advice can come later when our strength returns.

A study of 15,000 women found that 69 percent of women would rather talk to their best friends when unhappy than to their spouses. That is not a put-down; that is just the way it is.

Do you see your friendships as a ministry? So often we confine ministry to what we do at church. We think of friendship as an extra relationship when we are free from any expectations. I want to tell you that ministry and friendship *can* mix. Every day we are teaching those with whom we are associated. There are others who look to you for counsel, affirmation, and guidance. Do they find it easier to do right than wrong when they are around you? That is another thing about my good friend. She makes me want to do better. She makes me think higher thoughts when I am with her, and that is the influence we ought to have. Seek out those who challenge you to be your best. Teaching our children what to look for in a friend, and placing them in environments where such people can be found, is a gigantic contribution to the stability of their beliefs and values.

One of the costliest mistakes we can make is to make a non-Christian or a weak Christian our best friend. I've noticed how often my own behavior is a reflection of those with whom I spend my time. We can't live in a perfect world, and we need to help others and disciple them, but I am talking about that "best" friend. It is up to us to decide how close our fellowship will be with those who have thrown off moral restraints and whose life-style is anti-God. The reason is that we become like those with whom we associate. If your best friend is a weak Christian, she can have a profound influence on you and it isn't always for good. We seldom escape all the evil effects of such a relationship. No one can expect to maintain spiritual strength and growth if the values of our closest associates are not Bible-based.

What is the difference between a good friend and a best friend? The best friend is one with whom you have a deep rapport—one you would consider a real soul mate, a kindred spirit. Aristotle said, "Friendship is a single soul living in two bodies." When you have a best friend, you just think alike.

My friend Era and I always exchange Christmas presents. One Christmas when we lived in Texas, her Christmas present came in the mail, and it was as light as a feather. When I picked up that box, I thought, "Uh-oh!" I had sent her a package, about the same size, and it was as light as a feather. Yes, we sent each other the same gift! It was one of those silver phone covers with your name on it that fits on top of the old-fashioned phones. Landrum still has it in his office. This is the sort of bonding I am talking about.

Be a mentor to a younger friend. Span the generations. I don't know what I would have done without those who have been mentors for me. "A mentor is someone further on down the road from you who is going where you want to go, and is willing to give you some light to help you get there." Our job is to throw out little rays of light to help lead others through the darkness. When you are kind to someone, you hope he or she will be kind to someone else and it will become like a wildfire and spread.

One lady on her fortieth birthday wrote a mentor friend of hers to thank her for her friendship. She said, "Seeing you turn the next corner as I am turning mine, makes the one ahead seem much more natural and not so overwhelming."

I remember a friend in our last pastorate who had been on the pulpit committee. Her children were just a little older than mine. They were enough older than mine that she became a model for me in parenting. I remember well the day my oldest son came home and I found chewing tobacco in his back pocket. I was *devastated*. Never did I think a child of mine would carry chewing tobacco, much less chew it. I thought I was going to die. I remember asking my friend, "Jackie, did Joe ever do that?" She said, "Oh, Jo Ann, all the time." She was a classy lady and I said, "What did you do?" She said, "I just finally came to the conclusion that chewing tobacco smelled better than marijuana!" That sounds like a ridiculous story, but at the time it helped me tremendously. It helped me understand this was not the worst thing that could happen. I have since learned there are worse evils to fight and worse struggles to contend with. Yes, we need mentors.

We were on a flight not long ago from New Orleans to Phoenix and the weather was terrible. The pilot came on the intercom to apologize for the rough flight. Then he said something that captured my attention. He said, "We normally fly this portion of the trip at 34,000 feet but a plane flying 50 miles ahead of us has advised there is smooth air at 31,000 feet so we will begin our descent."

What a great illustration of what I'm talking about. There are going to be many on life's journey experiencing turbulence. They may be flying too high or have drifted off course, and need a mentor further on down the road pointing them in the right direction. Are you helping shape someone's faith? A teacher is one from whom someone else learns.

A pastor and his son were climbing an unfamiliar path up Rattlesnake Mountain in North Carolina. Tired and wondering if they were lost, they stopped to rest. A couple coming down the mountain happened along. The pastor asked them how much farther it was to the top.

They replied it was not far, adding that it was just a few hundred feet and then a short, steep climb. Smiling, they said, "You can make it, and the view will be worth the effort."

That was all the encouragement the pastor and his son needed to complete their climb.

Sometimes the climb becomes so fatiguing and discouraging that we might think of giving up. Sometimes our path becomes so dim or confusing we may wonder if we are hopelessly lost. At such times, a word of encouragement from a Christian friend can enable us to move on to fulfill God's will for our lives. Paul the apostle commanded us, "Therefore, encourage one another and build each other up" (1 Thess. 5:11 RSV).

A woman's ability to sustain herself in older years depends on her capacity for constructing a network of friends. A market research firm in New York City says, "The number of people aged 50 and older is expected to increase 76 percent by the year 2020, while the number under age 50 will decrease 1 percent, according to the Census Bureau." In addition, women live an average of seven years longer than men according to sociologist Beth B. Hess.

In 1965, about 30 percent of widows aged eighty-five and older lived alone, according to Christine MacDonald at the University of Southern California. However, 60 percent of these lived alone in 1990, and three out of four nursing-home residents are women. When we are left, we are going to survive only because we have established a network of friendships.

This is not to say that intimacy is not risky. It is risky. Intimacy is nothing but "in-to-me-see." When you let people in, you are laying yourself open to some risk and there are those even in our Baptist churches who may betray such confidence. That is why I am glad Susanne found a friend across the street who went to another church. Sometimes that is even better, especially in ministry.

When our oldest son moved to Phoenix, he knew only a few people and we didn't know anybody out there. We warned him about becoming transparent with people in his church too quickly. Only time reveals how much we can trust people. If we trust people as true friends, we want them to be trustworthy.

Be an initiator of friendships and understand up front that adult friendships are more difficult to start and harder to keep than childhood friendships. They take forethought, work, and effort as does any other worthwhile endeavor. You may have to be the one who invites a friend to lunch. Don't sit around as many do waiting for others to make the first move. A lot of people are afraid of close friendships. They may be shy or have been hurt by someone in the past.

I had a Catholic neighbor in Gulfport, Mississippi, who had been a good friend of the former preacher's wife. She was very "standoff-ish" when I came. I found out later she had been extremely hurt when her friend moved, so she was determined not to get close to another friend so she wouldn't be hurt again. There are a lot of reasons why people act as they do. Even on our campus we have those who never initiate any social gathering. Even though I am an initiator, I am not going to keep on initiating when favors are never returned. That is why I sometimes liken friendship to playing ball. It is impossible to play catch if one person refuses to throw the ball back. I'm not suggesting "counting" times. I am suggesting being an active participant in an important relationship. If you never throw the ball back, there is a limit to what one can do. Don't always expect to be on the receiving end. Be the "giver" sometimes.

I really have little patience in ministry with those who accept, accept, and accept but never give. People in Baptist churches are so incredibly generous to you. They give you meals, Christmas gifts, and all kinds of remembrances. You may not be able to repay "in kind," but you can do thoughtful little things for them from time to time. Don't ever take your blessings for granted when it comes to friendship. Loving, caring friendships are treasures from God.

PRAYER

Thank You for the handful of faithful friends who carried me through this experience and help me be the kind of person who is not only good to others, but good for them, too!

Questions for Chapter 8

1) In what ways have your friends strengthened you during your journey?

2) What kind of relationships do you typically build with friends? Draining relationships? Neutral relationships? Replenishing relationships? How can you develop friendships that renew you?

3) Read Ruth 3:1-18 and describe the special relationship between Ruth and Naomi. Do you have any intimate friends like that?

CHAPTER 9

Journey to Faith

PAUL SAID IN PHILIPPIANS we are to "work out our own salvation." When I first read that I was puzzled because the Bible also says, "not of works." Salvation is a gift but this means we are to take responsibility for our own spiritual growth. Don't look to your spouse or any other family member to spoon-feed you. Growth happens when we get serious about our own growth and do something about it.

This acrostic spelling "inner fire" may help us remember some important truths concerning our spiritual journey. Begin with the letter *I*.

Invest the Time

I know what you are saying: "I don't have any time. Between my job, family, and church I don't have any time to get alone with God." All I can say to that is: *we do what we want to do*. If you don't have time, pray for a "want to." In Phil. 2:13 God promises to give us that. "For it is God which worketh in you both to will and to do of His good pleasure." Ask Him to put into your heart a desire to grow. Crises are coming. How ready are you going to be?

We live such selfish life-styles, involved only with ourselves. We schedule tennis, bridge, aerobics, and shopping. We do numbers of other things and our culture contributes to this spirit. The world tells us to look out for "number one"—"we deserve it." As a result we have been brainwashed.

I just read a hair-color ad that said, "Isn't it time you did something for yourself? You can get your legs waxed, your hair highlighted or permed or your feet pampered in less than an hour now that salons across the country are catering to busy women." When we do have a little time we treat ourselves to some of these things. Is it possible that we are investing more in personal pleasure than in pleasing God? How much better it would be for you and your well-being to get alone with God. Invest the time with Him. Our lives are so full of "us" and so little of the Holy Spirit. If this ever changes, it is going to take *time*.

Everyone needs times alone. Our solitude is one of the pleasures that only we can arrange. Someone said, "God does not have just a set of intimate friends." We can be as intimate with our Heavenly Father as we choose to be. His revelation is in direct proportion to the level of our submission to His lordship in our lives. He never wants to hide Himself; rather, He wants to show Himself to us. He chooses that all of us be His friends and share a relationship with Him. This close relationship comes when we invest the time. If we do not model respect for our own need for solitude, our children will never learn that they, too, deserve time alone.

Nourish Your Inner Life

Let's face it, this Holy Quest has some monotonous moments. Sometimes the monotony of a religious routine gets to us and we are tempted to give up. If we are honest, often we think, "I don't want to go to church today. I don't feel like studying my Bible. I don't want to teach my Sunday School class. I am tired of that." Has lethargy crept into your quiet time? Have you become spiritually sluggish? Be honest. You have had these thoughts and I have, too. However, when we do, it is a pretty good indication that boredom has set in. It is a signal that we need to think of some creative way to nourish our inner life.

I am always interested in new ideas. I heard one minister's wife say if she made a new resolution to get up early to be alone with the Lord it was as if her husband and children knew she was up. They immediately wanted to know where something was or wanted her to do something. She said she started going to her van, where nobody knew where she was. With some Christian music and her Bible or devotional book she spent a few quiet moments with Him. I thought that was a great idea.

I am to the place now where I don't have any little children at home. I thought that day would never come, but it has. I can go out on my breezeway, sit in my chair with all my books and journals around me, and have a wonderful time. My recent experience has rejuvenated my quiet time. I began to look forward to it.

Now don't misunderstand me—I had always read my "daily Bible readings" since I was a child. But the motivation was duty. I did it because I knew it was right. I can't say I ever looked forward to that time as I do now. There have been times when I could not get through my work fast enough to spend some time with my Lord. I love to be out of town now because when I am, I have much more time with Him. When I am at home, the demands cry out for attention. I drive through the gates of our campus and begin to see needs everywhere: "He didn't do that. She didn't do that. Why didn't they do this?" I immediately get in gear. When I am out of town the opposite is true. I can put it in neutral. Be creative and do something that nourishes your inner being.

Another ingenious thing a student wife suggested to me was a "God's Provision" notebook. When you become aware of God's provision for you, write it down in your notebook. It is amazing how much clearer the "coincidences" in life become. When God provides finances when you didn't know how you were going to stay in school, enter that in your "God's Provision" notebook. We go through life saying, "Wasn't it nice that happened? Wasn't it a coincidence that it took place right then?" No! That is the Lord. He is providing for you.

I told every one of my children to get a "God's Provision" notebook. Mothers can tell children what to do, but we have no assurance they do it. However, I went to my daughter's home when she had just remodeled her kitchen. She called and said, "Mama, I have my Bible study group meeting with me and I need you to come help me get my house in order." I went to help her do all the things only mothers will do. I was dusting her night table and guess what I saw? Her "God's Provision" notebook. It thrilled me to death!

Another thing I kept during my illness was a journal. I had always intended to start a spiritual journal but kept putting it off. I had heard people tell of the blessing of "journaling," but I had never made the effort to do it. During my illness I began this spiritual discipline. What a rewarding experience it has been. When the Lord speaks to you or you read a promise, enter it in your journal.

It will help clarify your thoughts and remind you of God's ever-present help and love. A spiritual journal may be just the tool the Lord could use to nourish your inner life. Barbara Johnson suggests, "If we feed our faith, our doubts will starve to death."

Negate Your Rights

Acknowledge God's ownership of your life. In 1 Cor. 6:19-20 it says:

> What! Know ye not that your body is the temple of the HolyGhost which is in you, which ye have of God, and ye are not your own? For ye are bought with a price: therefore glorify God in your body, and in your spirit, which are God's.

Strong-willed disobedience is widely practiced—even toward God. It reminds me of the rural fellow with suspender-back overalls when he was asked if he took orders for firewood. His reply was, "I do have firewood and I sometimes sell it—but I don't take orders from nobody!" More than we like to admit, this could be a commentary on our times.

Believers don't have any rights. We turned all those over to Him when we were saved. "God does all things right and God has a right to do all things" is a truism. I will also tell you practicing faith like that is the *hardest* thing you will ever do. I finally came to this conclusion: "Lord, I don't understand about brain cells, but You do. You made me and You know everything about my body. You can open my blood vessels or close them as You see fit." We don't have any rights, and when we turn our lives over to Him the stress level goes down. We are not in charge anymore. He is in charge. We deserve nothing. He owes us nothing, yet He gives us everything. Acknowledge His ownership; negate your rights.

The Example of Jesus Should Teach Us

If we are going to be like Jesus, we must pray. Taking quiet time seemed to be one of His habits. Matt. 14:23 states: "And when He had sent the multitudes away, He went up into a mountain apart to pray: and when the evening was come, He was there alone." The emphasis is on privacy, being alone. He withdrew by Himself. His disciples were so intrigued by this that they asked Him to teach them how to pray. "Our Father, . . ."

Someone said, "This is a time to wash our souls in silence." Someone else said, "It is a time to climb up on God's lap and sit awhile." I could relate to that because all my energies were spent. I could not do anything but sit on His lap and be His child. I'm finding out that is okay—which leads to the next letter of our acrostic.

Rely on God's Strength

You cannot do anything alone. Rely on God. One thing this will do is free you from the perplexity of choosing your own path. I have never made decisions well. You just ask any member of my family and they will tell you this. I make them a little better than I used to, but I still am not good at it. Maybe that is one reason why I can relate to this thought. Wouldn't you like to be free from making the decisions in your life? I would, and we *can be free* when we turn it all over to Him and let Him make those decisions for us. Let Him put us on the right path and guide us in the very best possible way.

I-N-N-E-R. Invest the time. Nourish the inner life. Negate your rights. The example of Jesus is our pattern. Rely on God's enabling strength. If we follow these guidelines, we will have something to draw on when those hard times come. We will be strengthened for the crises of life.

Forward Movement

Paul said frequently, "I press on." "I pursue." "I follow after." He is simply saying to us, "Keep on keeping on." Sometimes we become impatient with our Christian growth. Just when we think we are maturing, something damages our Christian witness and we go back to "square one" spiritually. But remember also that, as we pray, honor Christ, follow Him, and love Him, something else happens. By our willingness Christ begins reaching deeper and deeper into our lives and *reworking us.* Slowly we become more kind, more caring, and more forgiving. What has Jesus done in your life recently? What has He done that you knew was of Him?

Karen Maines, a Christian author, calls this the "God-hunt." I'm not sure I care for that phrase because God is the one who "seeks and saves." He is the One always seeking us. However, there are other Scriptures that tell us: "If you truly seek Him, you will find Him." She encourages us to hunt for God in the normal day-to-day experiences of our lives. Can you look back and see how God has worked in your life? Are you more tuned in to His presence this year than last year? Many people go through life without this quality of recognition. Do you recognize God's hand at work in your life? He is so gentle that sometimes when I move at His instruction, I claim the achievement as my own. God is doing far more than we normally recognize. Open your eyes, mind, heart, and see—see what God is doing.

I never cease to be amazed at His care for me even in the mundane matters of life. Recently I was in Birmingham, Alabama with Landrum for a meeting, staying at the Sheraton Hotel. He gave me explicit instructions to a nearby mall—go out of the driveway, turn left on Highway 280 to I-459 and then left. He said that when I came to the first exit I would see the mall on the left.

We rehearsed the directions several times because of my past history. As Patsy Clairmont says, when I was being "knit together, somebody dropped my directional stitches!"

I got in the car, drove to the end of the driveway, and for some unknown reason decided against the mall trip. When Landrum came in from his meeting and found out I had not been shopping, he decided to take me. We went out of the driveway, turned left on Highway 280 to I-459, and took a left. We were soon passing the first exit, and I said, "I thought that is where you told me to turn." He said, "I made a mistake; it must be the next exit."

You have to understand, my husband never makes mistakes when it comes to highway numbers and directions. He is a walking atlas! Had I made that trip alone, even if I did not see a mall, it would *never* have occurred to me not to take that particular exit. Needless to say, by the time I discovered the mistake I probably would have been in Mobile!

Now, my question to you is, what turned me around on my initial trip? For those engaged in the God-hunt, a better question would be Who turned me around? I believe it was none other than the Lord Himself. The time was when it would not have occurred to me that God was directing this activity, but forward movement or growth in Christ opened my eyes.

Someone has called these "burning bush" experiences. These can be times when the Lord invites us to "turn aside and see" or "report for further instructions." My prayer became, "Lord, teach me to find burning bushes everywhere—at work, at play, at home, in the car, at the store. When I find one, teach me to worship. When I worship, teach me how I might serve You more effectively." I believe this is a step of forward movement, leading to greater growth.

I like this account of what one family did on a week's vacation in the picturesque Yosemite Valley. Each day they hiked to the water-falls, swam in the rivers, looked for deer, and ate fun food. Every night they played a game called "I Spy," when each family member had to record twenty ways he or she saw God working that day. They came up with a miraculous description of a waterfall, or per-haps they talked about a conversation with a new friend who was camping nearby. A fun vacation week turned into a meaningful spiritual experience, and a forward step in growth.

Make it fun to be a follower of Jesus. Jim Rayburn, the founder of Young Life, was fond of saying, "It's a sin to bore a kid with the gospel." That's why my family likes the idea of building beautiful memories with a spiritual theme. Ask the Lord to slacken your pace of life enough for you to discern the "burning bushes" when they appear.

A song says:

> When the valley is deep
> When the mountain is steep
> When the body is weak
> In Jesus' name *press on.*

Integrity

The Scripture says in Isa. 59:2, "But your iniquities have separat-ed between you and your God, and your sins have hid His face from you, that He will not hear." Does God hear you when you pray? If you confess your sins He is faithful and just to forgive you, but He will not hear if there is iniquity in your life.

Ps. 66:18 says, "If I regard iniquity in my heart, the Lord will not hear me." But 1 Pet. 3:12 says, "For the eyes of the Lord are over the righteous, and His ears are open unto their prayers: but the face of the Lord is against them that do evil."

If we are confessed up to date, if we are clean vessels, the Lord has promised to hear. That promise is valid *only* when our beliefs balance our behavior—when our conduct matches our convictions. Temptation will not leave us. We have to leave it! I agree with Leonard Ravenhill, who said, "A sinning man will stop praying. A praying man will stop sinning." Our faith must be an everyday, all-day-long life-style, not something we slip into on Sunday morning. Someone said, "Your private life does not entitle you to private sins."

There is nothing that negates our witness as quickly as known sin in our lives. There are examples everywhere, and the world can't wait to see a Christian fall because this eases their guilt. If our public and private lives do not mesh, integrity is lacking. What really interferes with our worship is the inconsistency between our claim to faith and our daily life. Christian growth is a process and takes *time* to work. The two things necessary for that growth to take place are:

> 1) refusing to be permissive toward evil things that destroy character;
> 2) continuing to serve Christ faithfully.

Churches are destroyed and people's lives are ruined by failing in these two areas; they may never recover. Sin never involves only the sinner—it has social as well as individual consequences. I'm confident this is the reason the Scripture says, "Watch and pray" (Matt. 26:41).

Leaders in the church today are saying if we are to win our world to Christ, we must recover our credibility, which has been so sadly weakened and badly tarnished by church people. The hell-bound world is skeptical due to glaring failures among prominent ministers and due to our political infighting. It is sad when people equate my faith with that of fallen TV evangelists, but they do. They are repulsed before I get a change to defend my beliefs. We make more headlines with our immorality than by our

Christlikeness. Others are saying we have freedom of speech—the right to say whatever we like. However, no one is required to listen. No one is obligated to tune us in, and anyone can tune us out at any time. To be listened to requires integrity. If you'd like others to hear, you back it up with your life. Don't be a detriment to the spread of the gospel. It's true that Christians listen too little, talk too much, and live lives that contradict what they say.

Even the strongest of us can succumb to the weakness of the flesh. Some wrong fascinates every man ("all have sinned," Rom. 3:23). If we nurture that base desire it will become an action.

Humans are by our very nature tempted to color outside the lines or explore the outer edges of what we know to be right behavior for a Christian. We convince ourselves we can handle these sins, and before we know it, we have self-destructed. When you think you are immune, you are in *big* trouble because temptation walks in the door that is left ajar! Watch and pray. Be alert. A person who doesn't want to fall shouldn't walk in slippery places. Temptations come even to Spirit-led persons. No one ever becomes so spiritual as to be beyond temptation. The devil would like nothing better than to destroy your marriage and your ministry. Don't let him do it.

Years ago when I was teaching a lesson on David and Bathsheba, I went home and got right up in Landrum Leavell's face. I said, "Let me tell you something, if it can happen to David it can happen to anybody." The higher your position (David was a king), the fewer people there are who dare to criticize you in any way, but God allows man to reap the results of his free choice. Don't let your guard down. Refuse to let sin clutter up your life. Keep your integrity and the Lord will hear you and bless your family as a result. "The just man walketh in his integrity: his children are blessed after him" (Prov. 20:7). Integrity and consistency have a powerful effect on every facet of your daily life. Personal morality is one of our most precious possessions and too important to be treated lightly.

JOURNAL ENTRY

"But after Uzziah became powerful, his pride led to his downfall" (2 Chron. 26:16 NIV®).

Nothing corrupts like power, and it is so sad when one whom You have trusted fails You. Lord, help Landrum and me to stay honest, and never to take advantage of our position in leadership. Already be preparing the ones to take our place who will have the same sense of integrity and purpose.

Refuse to Give Up

Your entire life is a work in progress. The beginning is behind you and the end is before you. Your responsibility is to make the best possible use of what God has given you that you possibly can. If you miss a day with your quiet time or even a week, just start over again. Read the Bible as if it were a letter from someone you loved, and treat Jesus' words as if they were personally directed to you. Refuse to give up.

The Expectation of Jesus, Not of Others, Should Motivate You

Ministers' wives are especially guilty of doing things because of the expectations of church members. As much as I think you ought to listen to others, the first consideration must be the expectation of Jesus and not your friends or even family. All women have a problem here because there is nobody who tries harder to meet the expectations of others than women. We spend our lives pleasing others. We are constantly looking outside for validation. We don't need to look outside; we need to look up.

Often Jesus' expectations for us may not be as high as others'. He knows we are weak. He made us vessels of clay. We need only please Him. How is it with you? Are you tending the inner fire?

I—Invest the time.
N—Nourish your inner life.
N—Negate your rights.
E—follow the Example of Jesus.
R—Rely on God's strength.

F—engage in Forward movement.
I—preserve your Integrity.
R—Refuse to give up.

E—be motivated by the Expectation of Jesus.

The story is told that at one time the famous pearls of the House of Austria lost their luster. A wise expert sank those pearls for months in the sea from which they came. As a result, they recovered their beauty and their radiance. So we need daily immersion in fellowship with the Living Lord. This will restore our luster to be able to give to those who depend on it. "Tend the inner fire so others can share the warmth."

Standing v. Saving Faith

Faith is a state of mind that enables one to face hardship or disaster with confidence in God and resolution. This kind of faith I have chosen to call "standing faith," as opposed to the "saving faith" discussed in chapter two. When the journey is too much for you, this is the faith that will see you through the valleys of life.

What is a valley? It is simply a depression between two mountains, but often where the battles of life are fought. Standing faith is not always getting what I want, or having things work out as I planned, but believing God and holding on to Him in the hard, hard places of life no matter what happens. It is the kind of faith that stands still when you feel like falling and believes what God has done and will do.

JOURNAL ENTRY

I have thought I was doing better, but this morning I'm back to the tears, the worry, and the uncertainty. Landrum says I've been praying for the wrong thing—I've prayed so hard for peace in this struggle. He says, pray for faith. Please, Lord, help me to think more positively, to have faith in Your perfect will, and to trust You with whatever my problem is or whatever the future holds. I wish You had given me something broken that could be fixed. Brain waves can't be fixed with surgery or a pill, but You are God and have never let me down yet. If this is what Your will is for me, help me to accept it and glorify You in it. And please return my joy.

I don't want to be a recluse and morose. That is the way I

feel right now and I know that does not honor You. Change
my thinking and give me confidence in Your perfect plan.
Show me the way to set my sights on things above—I want to
demonstrate peace in the middle of the storm. Help me to
know there is no valley so low that You are not there!

My youngest son shared with me a testimony he heard from a fellow preacher. He told of the tragic death of his twelve-year-old
daughter, who suffered an aneurysm following a basketball game.
The grieving pastor quoted from Isa. 40:31: "But they that wait
upon the Lord shall renew their strength; they shall mount up with
wings as eagles, they shall run, and not be weary; and they shall
walk, and not faint." Then he stated, "At this point I am not soar-
ing, I am not running nor am I walking, but I *am standing* on His
promises and through His grace."

Since Scripture assures us that valley experiences are going to
come, how are we going to stand amidst the trials? In an emergency, are you going to freeze or face it with faith? I'm suggesting
that we devise a plan for getting out of the valley before it's needed. If you are strong and have not experienced any storms yet, for-
mulate a plan now to implement when the need arises. When the
storms sweep over us, we need deep roots. Desperate situations
require drastic action and call into activity the strongest qualities of
the soul. "God chooses what we go through, we choose how we go
through it."

My plan is simply this:

> RELY on God.
> RENEW regular worship.
> RESIST the devil.
> RESOLVE to let others help you.

Rely on God

When things seem hopeless, rely on the Lord! Whatever the
weather of your life—overcast days or stormy nights—He is the
source of strength and encouragement. The greatest moments of
growth usually come at the times you feel totally helpless.

Overcomers begin with one assumption above all others: God
knows what He is doing.

JOURNAL ENTRY

> I read two passages today—one on "keep on praying" and
> one on "keep on believing." The word *believe* means to "lean
> one's weight on." My problem continues to be trying to do
> things myself. Help me rely totally on You.

It is such a temptation to depend on ourselves. We become
aware that we don't have the full measure of strength, but we continue to vie for control over our lives. However, valley experiences
throw us back to absolute dependence on God. There is little pride
left in the true valley experiences. As my pastor once said, "They
will grind all the fluff out of your life."

Isa. 31:1 is downright scary.

> Woe to those who go down to Egypt for help,
> who rely on horses,
> who trust in the multitude of their chariots,
> and in the great strength of their horsemen,
> but do not look to the Holy One of Israel,
> or seek help from the Lord! (NIV®).

A modern-day paraphrase might be:

> Woe to those who go down to the bank for help,
> who rely on others,
> who trust in counselors because they are many,
> and in athletes because they are strong,
> but who do not look to the Holy One of Israel,
> nor seek the Lord!

There are those who believe faith is just for emotional cripples.
How quickly that tune changes in the valley! "There are few athe-
ists in cancer wards or unemployment lines," said an article in
Newsweek magazine (January 6, 1992).

Before the time comes, determine to rely on God. As we trust
Him, we learn that He is utterly reliable. Trusting in God's power

prevents panic. We will never understand all there is to know about God, but even if we did, all explanations are insufficient when you are the one in pain. Standing faith has the confident expectation that God will be the all-loving provider the Bible says He is, and that He knows what He is doing.

Even in areas of personal confidence, we need to train our brain to rely on God, remembering, "Christ in you is the hope of glory." Human ability can be a liability if we trust our own adequacy, resources, and talent—not relying on God. The only ability God requires is availability.

If you have been away from the Lord for any reason, this is the time to return and relinquish control of this "out-of-control" situation. Submit to the will of God. Fall back on your commitment to Him or admit your need of Him. This is too big for your meager strength.

JOURNAL ENTRY

I am confident this experience is going to usher in an unprecedented era of blessing. Help me to "let go" and follow You completely. Don't let my faith fail. Keep me from wandering from the foot of the cross. I really want to live by faith—so easy to promise, and so impossible, in my own strength, to do, but "I can do all things through Christ . . ." (Phil. 4:13). I don't have to do it alone.

One of my favorite songs is the one entitled "I Have Returned," by Marijohn Wilkin, with these words:

I have returned to the God of my childhood.
To the same simple faith as a child I once knew;
Like the prodigal son, I longed for my loved ones,
For the comforts of home and the God I outgrew,
I have returned to the God of my childhood;
Bethlehem's Babe the prophets' Messiah.
. . . I just heard a shout from the angels in glory,
Praising the Lord a child has come home.

When life is out of control, return to the Father. Even better is to recognize now our limitations and remain with God.

Renew Regular Worship

Do you endure church or enjoy it? Miserable people aren't always unsaved. Christians who have backslidden have just enough of the world in them to not really enjoy walking with the Lord, and just enough of God in them to not really enjoy sin, so they are in a tormented situation.

If you are not a joyful Christian, it says to me you are riding the fence. In my experience, I've observed that pagans and dedicated Christians are the happy ones. The pagans, at least temporarily, are usually enjoying life. They are good company. Sold-out Christians have an enviable serenity, but misery comes when we try to please the world and God. I know—I've tried. There is no peace there, no sparkle.

Corporate worship as well as daily communion with Him through Bible study and prayer are essential—whether you feel like it or not! We have a preacher friend who went through a terrible period of depression for no known reason. When he shared with me after his recovery, I asked, "What did you do?" He said, "Jo Ann, I just kept doing what I knew was right to do—worship, study of God's Word, prayer—even though I felt as if my prayers weren't getting any higher than the ceiling."

God is faithful and you don't have to understand prayer to practice it. Scripture says we "have not because we ask not." Contact with God is so simple, and we make it so difficult. Just "ask," and ask specifically. I'm afraid we talk more about prayer than we actually practice it.

Get close to the Lord when the dark days hit. As a Chinese proverb says, "Dig the well before you are thirsty." This requires communication. Make some impossible prayer goals and see God work. Great Christians are daring. A *dynamic* emerges when we are capable of believing the impossible, because then it does happen! What is it that makes us pull back and say, "Everything is possible for our Lord . . . but not that . . . or this!"? That then becomes the very thing we must trust to the Lord's limitless possibilities. As long as we operate in our strength we will never know "what a mighty God we serve."

Act on His Word. Don't deprive yourselves of your infinite resources by ignorance. Deal with what is not consistent with His will. Believe me, He will show you what you have to "let go of" to conform. It is our willingness to obey fully God's direction that assures us of His help.

If you have encountered hardships, you can assume that God knows you can handle them. God is faithful, and He is aware of every detail—past, present, and future. No event escapes His attention or is beyond our capacity to cope.

There are a thousand voices calling out for your attention and mine. The questions always arise, "How can I know if this is His will or my own? How can I know if the Lord is speaking to me?" My fear has always been that in the midst of so many voices clamoring for my attention, I would miss the Master's voice. Choosing to spend time regularly with God is our ultimate security for staying in His will. Through spending more time in fellowship with Him, we can begin to recognize the distinctiveness of His voice. This intimacy is developed over time. A quiet time every day turns our religious experience from weekly worship to a daily walk.

Scriptures were not originally written simply as materials to study, but as guides for the tortuous pilgrimage of life. From an old tract we read: "No, dear suffering child of God, you cannot fail if only you dare to believe, to stand fast and refuse to be overcome."

Resist the Devil

I never realized just how quickly those of us who are strong can become weak. And believe me, Satan has a field day with a weakened body! If you don't believe that, read about Elijah in 1 Kings 19. He was so discouraged he even requested to die. Yes, the devil likes nothing better than to hit us when we are down. He is always ready to take advantage of a time of weariness.

The first thing we must come to grips with is that he is real. Satan is a distinct personality who even tried to tempt our Lord. Expect to be hit by the enemy. My husband always says if you don't run into him every morning it could be you are going in the same direction! And Christians are more at risk for his advances than pagans because he already has them. Why would he waste time on those already living his lies?

Most of us are looking for sunny skies and smooth seas when what we really ought to expect is turbulence and storms. The tempter loves to fish in troubled waters. Someone said, "The best token of His presence is the adversary's defiance and the more real our blessing the more certainly it will be challenged." Satan has endeavored throughout all generations to thwart the plan of God, and he becomes more and more interested in you as you become more faithful. When we get serious about spiritual growth, the enemy gets serious about opposing us. Landrum always said that following any victory—good revival, successful stewardship campaign, or just harmony in the church—we could expect the worst. It seems when things are going well and our spiritual shields are down, we can expect disaster from Satan's darts.

We visited friends recently in Glen Rose, Texas. While there we attended the Passion play depicting the life of Christ. We have taken groups to see the world-famous play in Oberammagou, Germany on three occasions, yet I believe this one ministered to me in an even greater way than the German version. There must be a lesson there, too, about our penchant to equate excellence with distance and publicity. However, the play in Glen Rose was held in a giant amphitheater in that small Texas town and was well done.

The thing that impressed me the most was the red-costumed devil who was *ever present*. Most of the time he was in the background or flitting across the stage, but never far from the activities being depicted. The visual image reminded me anew that Satan is forever in the wings waiting to attack us when we least expect it, and are the most vulnerable.

Gordon MacDonald says a friend asked him this sobering question, "If Satan were to blow you out of the water, how do you think he would do it?" How would you answer that question? Chances are it would be in your area of greatest weakness, but never forget there is no safe place from his attacks except under the shadow of the Almighty. There *will* come a point in every person's spiritual experience where faith will be tested. Never try to resist the devil without God. Only His resources will see you through.

Max Lucado wrote concerning Satan:

> His commission from the black throne room is clear, and fatal: "Take nothing from your victim; cause him only to take everything for granted."

He'd been on my trail for years and I never knew it. But I know it now. I've come to recognize his tactics and detect his presence. And I'm doing my best to keep him out. His aim is deadly. His goal is nothing less than to take what is most precious to us and make it appear most common.

To say that this agent of familiarity breeds contempt is to let him off easy. Contempt is just one of his offspring. He also sires broken hearts, wasted hours, and an insatiable desire for more. He's an expert in robbing the sparkle and replacing it with the drab. He invented the yawn and put the hum in the humdrum. And this strategy is deceptive.

He won't steal your salvation; he'll just make you forget what it was like to be lost. You'll grow accustomed to prayer and thereby not pray. Worship will become commonplace and study optional. With the passing of time he'll infiltrate your heart with boredom and cover the cross with dust so you'll be safely out of reach of change. Score one for the agent of familiarity.

We are warned often in Scriptures about his aggressiveness. Peter likened him to a lion roaming about seeking those he may devour. We must not take this enemy for granted. Paul reminds us in Eph. 6:12-13 that "our struggle is not against flesh and blood, but against the spiritual forces of wickedness," and that we are to stand firm against the "schemes of the devil." We are told to be alert, to "armor up," and to appropriate the power of God and His word. Satan's doom is sure, and his vengeance is certain. The good news is that even if Satan turns up the heat, our Heavenly Father keeps His hand on the thermostat!

Resolve to Let Others Help You

Trust God—He has not abandoned you. "*Keep walking* and sooner or later God will send one of His servants to bless you," was the advice of one minister. When that happens, talk honestly about your feelings. Bottling up feelings is not only unhealthy; it prevents others from knowing us. Vulnerability draws people to us. Life is a team sport and we cannot do it alone. We are interdependent people, and God has given us a fabric of relationships to help us when the hard times come. Cultivate transparency and openness, and invite others to share your journey and give you company. Perhaps we can try "asking" for help and stop trying to do everything ourselves.

There are so many times we hit the unexpected hard places of life, and all the things we know about the Lord are jostled out of our minds and hearts. It is hard to step over that line and just trust God.

JOURNAL ENTRY

A staff member from Dauphin Way Baptist Church sent me this wonderful promise. "Let your hard days build sturdy character and reinforce your faith, you may not enjoy them, but they won't be wasted" (James 1:2-3, translation unknown).

I'm clinging to the fact that they won't be wasted. It is so hard to be patient during "God's silences." Of course, it wouldn't require any faith if I knew the end from the beginning. Give me more faith—in You, the doctors, the medicine, even in myself to get a handle on this. Help me not to brood and dwell on every little thing. Feelings are not reliable—You are! Perform in me the miracle of physical and emotional healing if it is Your will. I've taught for years—"You can't beat God's will for your life." Help me now to believe and live by the fact that Your way is best.

Build on the Rock of Jesus

When the Los Angeles area was racked by an earthquake in early 1994, many were depending on foundations that were not solid. How solid is your foundation? Everybody either has Jesus or needs Jesus. Can you survive a shaking? Either God is or God is not. If not, man is without hope. If God is, we better choose to believe in Him. Belief is the only possible foundation for a significant relationship. We must look upon God not just as a fire escape or life preserver, but as Savior and Friend. Maybe we need our boats rocked to get out of our apathy.

Where are you on your spiritual pilgrimage? Faith, in the last analysis, is a personal process. Do you have broad theorizing that proves useless in a real crisis? Overcoming happens only in manageable increments of time: daily, hourly commitment to practice these truths.

The Sermon on the Mount closes with a parable. In this parable Jesus spoke about the wisdom of hearing and obeying His teachings. Jesus compared one who hears His words and obeys them to a wise builder.

The wise person builds his home on a foundation of rock. This house may look just like those built on sand, but only because the foundation is hidden. Only the builder knows it is anchored on rock. Such a house can withstand rain, rising waters, and the gales that whip against it.

Isn't that a lovely picture for believers? We cannot be moved because our foundation stone is Jesus. Through Him we can remain standing against the rain of problems, the rising waters of disappointments, and the winds of Satan's temptations. In Him we can weather any storm that comes our way!

PRAYER

Lord, help me learn the lessons of faith when life is calm so I may be prepared when the winds of adversity rise up against me.

Questions for Chapter 9

1) Assess your "inner fire." Are you growing in your faith? How hot is your spiritual fire?

2) In your journey to faith, ask God to help you:
RELY on God.
RENEW regular worship.
RESIST the devil.
RESOLVE to let others help you.
What was His response to you?

3) Read the Sermon on the Mount (Matt. 5-7). What did Jesus say about those who obey His teachings?

CHAPTER 10

Dark-Journey Promises

ANOTHER CERTAINTY OF MINE has to do with God's unchanging Word and its all inclusive promises. These biblical assurances provided me with encouragement that has sustained me in my journey. "That ye be not slothful, but followers of them who through faith and patience inherit the promises" (Heb. 6:12).

When I think of promises, I automatically think of Abraham. Abraham was so in tune with God that he knew His voice. He recognized God's voice because he had walked with God for some time before sensing His call. He went out "not knowing whither he went," but God promised to make of him a great nation. No wonder Abraham has been called the "father of the faithful."

In fact, God's call to Abraham to leave his home for an unknown destination in Gen. 12:2-3 provided *six* promises:

1) I will make you a great nation.
2) I will bless you.
3) I will make your name great.
4) You will bless them that bless you.
5) You will curse them that curse you.
6) In you shall all the families of the earth be blessed.

To remind us that there is a human response expected, God included a command—". . . thou shalt be a blessing." The blessed person is always responsible to be a blessing!

Abraham must have sat for the following portrait of faith. Faith is "contentment to sail with sealed orders because of our confidence in the Admiral—fearing nothing while He is with you." A step-at-a-time obedience has been the experience of many a believer. Nothing is clearer in the Bible than the guarantee of divine guidance to anyone who seeks it.

Promises are a source of *joy*. Every day of your life can be God-planned and directed. God desires and delights in directing the lives of His children. We, as Christians, are *never* promised exemption from the whirlwinds—just an everlasting foundation. I have to remember that He has a plan for my life, even when I am experiencing severe setbacks and can't understand His reasons.

I had a letter from a precious friend written while she was taking those horrible treatments for cancer. She wrote: "This has been a shocking experience for all of us, but we are learning again that God prevents trouble but *not always,* God delivers from trouble, but *not always.* God sustains through trouble and *always.*" She later died, but with serenity and peace. Faith does wonderful things. Sometimes it heals; sometimes it changes the situation; then sometimes it brings the assurance and security we need to face what lies before us.

Scripture has a marvelous way of ministering to us during times of crisis. Trust in God's Word is all that brought me through this major crisis in my life. Often we have to look beyond the events of the moment, and hang on to the promises of God with confidence in the fact that He still holds the controlling reins of our lives. Even if the rest of life unravels, His Word holds strong. God is trustworthy and *will* keep His promises. We must lean not so much on promises as on the *Promiser.* Ask Him to give you a word from His Word for the need of your heart today.

JOURNAL ENTRY

> I have been extremely nervous this morning and the back of my neck is tight and aches. It doesn't do to dwell on my feelings. I'm trying to "think on good things." Ps. 34 has blessed me today—every verse. It promises that He hears and answers, knows our tears, has angels camped about us, and that the Lord is nigh unto those with a broken heart. What promises! Help me to claim these, accept whatever the future holds, and believe with trust "the Lord is not far from me" (Ps. 35:22).

We sing lustily the hymn "Standing on the Promises" when most of us are shaking on the premises! ". . . When the howling storms of doubt and fear assail, by the living Word of God I shall prevail." My friend, let me tell you from experience, that is the *only way* you will survive—the Bible is the only true anchor in the storms of life.

The Scripture goes on to say about Abraham, "After he had patiently endured, he obtained the promise" (Heb. 6:15). Oh, why did it have to say that?! I don't like either one of those words—*patient* or *endure*. I'm an action-oriented person and I want things done *now*. Lest you ever think I have it all together, let me burst that bubble *quickly*. I still fight the battle daily of a lack of faith and trust in Him.

Do you ever pray for patience? *Don't.* I quit that years ago when my children were small. If anybody ever needs patience it is a mother of four preschoolers, and for a long time, that was my constant prayer. Then I studied the book of James, and found out how you get patience, and it *only* comes through trials and tribulations. That ended my "patience prayers."

JOURNAL ENTRY

It is amazing how teachable we get with a little pain. My uncomfortable circumstances are not invisible to God. Let God be God! Ruth Graham says the Lord taught her to "quit studying the problems and start studying the promises." Worship and worry cannot live in the same heart; they are mutually exclusive. I'm confident He will lead me out of the darkness and into His marvelous light. True patience is the losing of our self-will in His perfect will.

ANOTHER JOURNAL ENTRY

I think I found my problem today when I read this quote. "Your desire for the things you wish is perhaps stronger than your desire for the will of God to be fulfilled in its arrival." Obviously, what I want is still stronger than what God wants. I've always preached that you can't beat God's will for your life. Why can't I practice that? I'm trying to rest in the promise that God is fitting all this together and that His will governs all. Haven't I wanted His will all these years? Why am I bucking now? Increase my faith and help me understand that *he who suffers most, has the most to give!* Faith's eyes don't always know the reason *why*, but faith and trust do not need to know why.

Lessons Learned

The first time I spoke following "my sabbatical," I talked on "lessons from the fire." I reminded my audience, even as I remind you, that many others have been overwhelmed by sorrows, difficulties, trials, and illnesses far worse than I have known. I can't speak for them, but only of God's provision for *me*. However, should you be in the fire now, let me give you a verse to cling to:

> When you go through deep waters and great troubles, I will be with you. When you go through rivers of difficulty, you will not drown! When you walk through the fire of oppression, you will not be burned up—the flames will not consume you (Isa. 43:2 TLB).

Isn't it a comfort to know that even in our sinking moments, our "wit's end" moments, God is there with an outstretched hand to keep us from going under?

Did you know "wit's end" was in the Bible? I didn't until I found this *wonderful* promise. Ps. 107:27-28 says, "They reel to and fro, and stagger like a drunken man, and are at their wit's end. Then they cry unto the Lord in their trouble, and He bringeth them out of their distresses."

I remember so well when I discovered it because we were on a trip in the car. I promptly asked Landrum if he knew "wit's end" was in the Bible, and his reply was, "Which translation?" I took great pride in telling him King James since he is definitely a "King James man"!

JOURNAL ENTRY

Lord, I know my limitations and circumstances are not a surprise to you. You have everything under control. Help me soar above my limited mobility, and have faith in Your *promises* to bring good from it all.

The Bible speaks of "fire" experiences in many places:

"The fire shall try every man's work of what sort it is" (1 Cor. 3:13).

"That the trial of your faith . . . though it be tried with fire might be found unto praise and honor and glory at the appearing of Jesus Christ" (1 Pet. 1:7).

"Did ever people hear the voice of God speaking out of the midst of the fire, as thou hast heard and live?" (Deut. 4:33).

"Out of heaven He made thee to hear His voice, that He might instruct thee: and upon earth He showed thee His great fire and thou heardest His words out of the midst of the fire" (Deut. 4:36).

The deepest lessons come out of the deepest waters and hottest fires! Why? We find the answer in Deut. 4:35: "Unto thee it [the fire] was shown, that thou mightest know that the Lord He is God, there is none else beside Him."

We are perhaps more open to hearing God's voice in trouble than any other time. I'll confess—I never have heard God speak to me audibly. In fact, I asked a precious friend how she knew when a promise in the Bible was just for her. Her advice was, "Just read and when you feel one speak directly to you—*claim it!*" Read until you find something that touches your heart and answers whatever need is most pressing for you today. When that happens, you will know it and know, too, how to act on it. If you have gotten a "sure word" of promise, take it implicitly and trust it absolutely.

This may be likened to a self-opening gate. As we move forward expectantly, the gate responds. The promises of God are like that gate. We move forward by faith and God responds in fulfillment of His promises.

I tried that, and it worked! There were two promises I claimed as my very own. One assured me I wasn't going to die, and the other encouraged me that I would get better. Ps. 118:17-18: "I shall not die, but live, and declare the works of the Lord. The Lord hath chastened me sore: but He hath not given me over unto death."

Ps. 71:20: "Thou, which hast shown me great and sore troubles, shall quicken me again, and shall bring me up again from the depths of the earth." "A new heart also will I give you: and a new spirit will I put within you" (Ezek. 36:26). I've come to agree with the one who said, "I have never heard Jesus speak audibly. He speaks louder than that."

My husband gives this account:

One of my most unforgettable and beloved professors was Dr.

J. Wash Watts, who taught Hebrew and Old Testament at New Orleans Baptist Theological Seminary. He had served as a missionary to Palestine in his early ministry. His teaching included numerous experiences from his days in the Middle East, but one in particular has continued to bless me. He described the scene at the noon hour when a number of shepherds would bring their flocks and congregate at one of the scarce watering spots in that dry, arid land. The dust would be billowing upward and the sheep would become hopelessly intermingled. He wondered how they could ever separate them into the individual flocks again. When the time of refreshment was over, one shepherd would move out on a hillside, another on top of a pile of rocks, and others in different directions. Each would give his own unique call or whistle. Unerringly and immediately every sheep would move in the direction of the familiar sound, and without error every sheep would follow his own shepherd and join his own flock. In John 10:27 Jesus said, "My sheep hear My voice, and I know them, and they follow Me."

JOURNAL ENTRY
(July 28, 1991, my thirty-eighth wedding anniversary)

I found another *wonderful* promise today. "They that dwell under His shadow shall return; they shall revive as the corn and grow as the vine . . ." (Hos. 4:7). I have finally come to the place where I know there is nothing dependable but *You*. Help me continue to listen for Your will, and to remember it is the very time for faith to work when sight ceases. Moses found that out. The Scripture says in Exod. 20:21 that Moses drew near unto the thick darkness where God was. It is such a comfort to know You are in the dark places with us, and when we feel the loneliest and most forsaken You are still there.

I wrote the next day:

We are in the mountains and it is so beautiful. There is something about the lofty peaks which remind me of *You*. But for every peak there is a valley. In my life and our thirty-eight years of marriage, we have had far more mountains than valleys. Thank You for that—and for trusting me with this valley.

God knows how much I can stand or He would not have given me this trial. He knows my strength and never goes beyond it.

Purposeful Testings

Our burdens are God-given. He knew my capacity before the plan was made. "The very fact of trial proves that there is something in us very precious to the Lord. . . . Christ would not test us if He did not see the precious ore of faith!" Not only did He promise not to give us more than we could stand (1 Cor. 10:13) but He promised that "our light affliction, which is but for a moment, worketh for us" (2 Cor. 4:17).

We were in Ruston recently with our good friends James and Dianne Davison for a family wedding. We met and visited with Mr. Ed Mitcham. Now anybody in North Louisiana knows about the famous Mitcham peaches! They are big, sweet, quality peaches, much in demand because of these known facts.

James and Dianne are sweet and generous enough to share these peaches with us and others on our campus each year, so we have a special interest in each crop. After several years of a slim harvest due to freezing weather late in the season, Landrum asked Mr. Mitcham how the peaches would be this year. He said something that hit me right between the eyes! He said, "Those freezes actually *help* us *and* our trees when they don't kill them."

He went on to explain the costly thinning process in the orchards. It takes a man at least an hour to thin a tree, and they have fifteen thousand to sixteen thousand peach, plum, and nectarine trees. You don't have to be a mathematician to figure out the expense involved in that procedure, plus they do what he called "preharvest pruning." They leave only one peach on each shoot, which explains the size and quality of his peaches.

According to Mr. Mitcham, those freezes were *forced thinning* and actually saved him money, time, and resulted in "his good." I'm sure at the time the end result of those "bad-weather experiences" was not known, but God worked it for *good*.

It also occurred to me, as he talked about leaving only one peach per shoot, that the apostle Paul was right on target when he said, "This *one* thing I do." Could it be we have small fruit because we have never engaged in preharvest pruning, leaving only one peach per shoot? Pruning *will* come, and isn't it wiser to narrow our focus and make some changes in our life-styles before change is forced upon us as mine was?

In God's management of the affairs of men, suffering is never senseless; rather, it is for us what pruning is to peach trees. We must trust the master Gardener to prune us with tenderness so we will bear the best fruit.

JOURNAL ENTRY

I continue to struggle with stress, but You are always faithful to give me a promise to hold on to. Today it was from Deut. 23:5: "...The Lord thy God turned thy curse into a blessing...." Lord, I lift up my whole situation that looms so threateningly today—my health, my family, retirement, and my future—to You. Turn it all into a blessing for Your glory.

All God's testings have a purpose, and you can assume that God knows you can handle them. James 1:2 in the Phillips translation reads: "When all kinds of trials and temptations crowd into your lives, my brothers, don't resent them as intruders, but welcome them as friends! Realize that they come to test your faith and produce in you the quality of endurance."

Someday we will see the light. All He asks now is that we trust Him—walk by faith and not by sight. Good can come from our fire experiences. Someone said, "What the caterpillar calls the end of the world, the Creator calls a butterfly." Trial is only for a season—showers soon pass. Our lives will soon be a sea of glass, and we'll be just as happy as now we are sorrowful. He that sends the clouds can as easily clear the skies. *Yea!*

When the next storm comes in your life, look at God's promises as an umbrella in hand. Learn to walk in the promises revealed in His Word. Ask God to give you *joy* in the storm, and watch for the rainbow that marks the end. It takes varying amounts of rain before the rainbow appears, so hang on!

JOURNAL ENTRY

My words for today are cease meddling with God's plans and will. Do not try to get out of the dark places, except in God's time and in God's way. It is better to walk in the dark with God than in the light alone. Give me the faith to go on, believing the promise to quicken me again when You see fit!

Some years ago we visited England, Scotland, and Ireland. One of the highlights was a trip to the factories that make fine china and renowned crystal. It was said that the finest china in the world is burned at least three times, some of it more than three times. Most fine china is always burned three times. Why so often? Three times are necessary so that the colors are brought out more beautifully and then fastened there to stay.

Humans are fashioned in this same way. Our trials are burned into us three times, and by God's grace these beautiful colors are there and there forever.

My Scriptures of Hope

I have compiled the following Scriptures to shine a light of hope during dark days. When there is a blank, personalize the Scripture with your own name!

"Do not fear for I have redeemed you, I have called you, _____, you are mine! When you pass through the waters, I will be with you, and through the rivers, they will *not* overflow you. When you walk through the fire, you will *not* be scorched, nor will the flame burn you, for I am the Lord your God, the Holy One of Israel, your Savior!" (Isa. 43:1-3 NAS).

"Thou, which has showed me great and sore troubles, shall *quicken me again,* and shall bring me up again from the depths of the earth" (Ps. 71:20).

"When all kinds of trials and temptations crowd into your lives, my brothers, don't resent them as intruders, but welcome them as friends! Realize that they come to test your faith and produce in you the quality of endurance" (James 1:2, translation unknown).

"Let Him have all your worries and cares, for He is always thinking about you and watching everything that concerns you" (1 Pet. 5:7 TLB).

"Don't worry over anything whatever; tell God every detail of your needs in earnest and thankful prayer, and the peace of God, which transcends human understanding, will keep constant guard over your hearts and minds as they rest in Christ Jesus" (Phil. 4:6-7 Phillips).

"In the day of my trouble I will call upon thee; for *thou wilt answer me*" (Ps. 86:7 NAS).

" . . . the God of all comfort, Who comforteth us in all our tribulation, that *we may be able to comfort them* which are in any trouble, by the comfort wherewith we ourselves are comforted of God" (2 Cor. 1:3b-4).

"What time I am afraid, I will trust in Thee" (Ps. 56:3).

"There hath no temptation taken you but such as is common to man: but *God is faithful,* Who will not suffer you to be tempted above that ye are able; but will with the temptation also make a way to escape, that ye may be able to bear it" (1 Cor. 10:13).

"What I tell you in darkness, that speak ye in light: and what ye hear in the ear, that preach ye upon the house tops" (Matt. 10:27).

"Now no chastening for the present seemeth to be joyous, but grievous: nevertheless, *afterward* it yieldeth the peaceable fruit of righteousness unto them which are exercised thereby" (Heb. 12:11).

"But our God is in the heaven; He hath done *whatsoever He hath pleased*" (Ps. 115:3).

"The righteous cry, and the Lord heareth, and delivereth them out of all their troubles. The Lord is nigh unto them that are of a broken heart" (Ps. 34:17-18a). (All of Ps. 34 is great.)

"He shall call upon me, and I will answer him; I will be with him in troubles; I will deliver him, and honor him" (Ps. 91:15). (All of Ps. 91 is great.)

"Be still, and know that I am God" (Ps. 46:10).

"O Lord my God, I cried unto Thee, and Thou hast healed me. O Lord, Thou hast brought up my soul from the grave: Thou hast kept me alive, that I should not go down to the pit. . . . Weeping may endure for a night, but *joy cometh in the morning*" (Ps. 30:2-3, 5).

"God is our refuge and strength, a very present help in trouble. Therefore will not we fear" (Ps. 46:1-2a). (All of Ps. 46 is great.)

"Though he fall, he shall not be utterly cast down: for the Lord *upholdeth him* with His hand" (Ps. 37:24).

"It is good for me that I have been affected, that I might learn thy statutes" (Ps. 119:71 NAS).

"Then they cried unto the Lord in their trouble, and He delivered them out of their distresses" (Ps. 107:6 NAS).

"I will lift up mine eyes unto the hills, from whence cometh my help. My help cometh from the Lord which made heaven and earth" (Ps. 121:1-2).

"Yea, though I walk through the valley of the shadow of death, I will fear no evil: for Thou art with me, Thy rod and Thy staff they comfort me" (Ps. 23:4).

"Hear me speedily, O Lord, my spirit faileth; hide not thy face from me, lest I be like unto them that go down into the pit. Cause me to hear Thy loving kindness in the morning, for in Thee do I trust: *cause me to know the way wherein I should walk;* for I lift up my soul unto Thee" (Ps. 143:7, 8). (All of Ps. 143 is great.)

"But I know, that even now, whatsoever thou wilt ask of God, God will give it thou" (John 11:22).

"He will not suffer thy foot to be moved; He that keepeth thee will not slumber. Behold, He that keepeth _____ shall neither slumber nor sleep" (Ps. 121:3-4).

"Fear thou not; for I am with thee: be not dismayed; for I am thy God: I will strengthen thee; yea, I will help thee; yea, I will uphold thee with the right hand of my righteousness" (Isa. 41:10).

PRAYER

Lord, fine-tune my ears to Your will today. Help me to be so attuned to the voice of God that even small failures in love that occur so easily cause me true remorse. Help me to look on this period as a "blessed inconvenience," and to know that you will look down upon all our lives, loves, and labors with *joy.*

Questions for Chapter 10

1) Read Gen. 12:2-3 and identify the six promises God gave to Abraham. Ask yourself how God has fulfilled these same promises in your life.

2) List below some lessons you have learned during a dark journey.

3) What God-given burdens are you carrying right now? How is He helping you to carry your burdens?

CHAPTER 11

Journey toward the Future

THE SIXTH CERTAINTY OF MINE is that God can control my future and yours. Most of us have 20/20 hindsight. We can see how God has worked in the past, but somehow we have trouble trusting Him with the present and with the future. The familiar hymn says, "Oh God, our help in ages past, our hope for years to come." Any relationship with God that does not give us confidence in forgiveness of sin, power for the present, and hope for the future is inadequate. I hope you have a faith sufficient to see you through it all. Andrae Crouch said, "Through it all, through it all, I have learned to trust in God."

The journey of life has often been likened to the seasons, spring being the buoyancy of youth who know no limits to their abilities and who travel the journey of life with a reserve of freshness and vigor. There are some problems, but these are insignificant in comparison to the joy of youthful living.

The birthdays continue and summer approaches. Responsibilities build with family and the constant financial crunch, but summer is also characterized by a carefree life, no school, little worry—no disturbing doubts to make them old inside. These are the ones who keep on believing, hoping, loving, and looking forward to every day of life.

Autumn approaches, which is the season of change. Foliage changes, weather changes, time changes, and it becomes a season of reflection. This is my favorite time of year with the frosty mornings, cool nights, riot of color in the leaves in many parts of the country, and the return to routine following the busy summer. These kinds of changes occur also in life. This is the season when the wrinkles begin, the hair color changes, the joints begin to sound like the Fourth of July, and there is more interest in your cholesterol numbers than your golf score. This is often called middle age.

Winter sets in with the short days and long nights. It is cold and barren, and you wonder if your soul is ever going to thaw. You are alone, depressed, and going through the fire. It is then we remember Jesus' words to the remnant of Israel: "And even to your old age I am He: and even to gray hairs I will carry you: I have made, and I will hear; even I will carry, and will deliver you" (Isa. 46:4).

It is said that there are four stages of life: 1) childhood, 2) youth, 3) young adulthood, and 4) "You look wonderful!" We know we have hit middle age or beyond when people say, "You look wonderful!" in place of "Hello!" That comment covers a multitude of gray hairs and wrinkles! But change is the name of the game and I'm learning we can't live the winter of life on the spring schedule.

Being able to enjoy the stage of life we are in is not easy. Life is an ongoing adjustment, and so much of life is lived in anticipation of the next stage. We are so tomorrow oriented that we do not enjoy the present. My advice in every season is look up! "Up . . . Is not the Lord gone out before thee?" (Judg. 4:14). Be still and discover anew, as I did, that He is God. Ron Dunn says, "You never know Jesus is all you need until Jesus is all you have!" It is not what I'll do, but what He'll do! "Our might is His almightiness."

I'm experiencing the autumn of life right now with all the changes occurring—frightening at times, but exciting. I want to take time to enjoy the deeper and more meaningful things of life. I want to see beyond the hardships and sorrows and catch a vision of the invisible.

That's what Moses did: ". . . For he endured, as seeing Him Who is invisible" (Heb. 11:27). His mind was not on himself and his chronological age, but on a dedication to a great cause. It gave him something to live for, kept him persevering through trials, defeats, sorrows, and kept him young at heart.

I want to stay "internally young" while the years slip away. The Bible speaks of this when it says, "But though our outward man perish, yet the inward man is renewed day by day" (2 Cor. 4:16). As physical strength gives way to the years, internally a person is only as old as he thinks. I don't want to enter into a "calendar neurosis," which is the dread of turning the calendar. I like the story of the lady who wouldn't tell her age, but said it was somewhere between menopause and large print! At least she kept her sense of humor.

When my mother would mention her birthday, age, or condition, Landrum always reminded her, "It sure beats the alternative!" It is "killing" to dwell on the idea of getting old, your usefulness waning. I fell into that trap, but no more. That is a dead-end street, and it makes us psychologically old regardless of the years.

I woke up to the fact recently that I am living in my favorite season. Why waste even one moment of these precious days?! Life becomes stale and boring to those who see no farther than self-interest, self-cares, and self-gratification. I don't want to live life full of anxiety, fretfulness, and weariness. I want excitement, zest, and a new spark to characterize my life for each new milestone in my journey.

Advantages of Aging

I'm trying to dwell on the numerous advantages of aging. Some I have discovered are:

1) Schedules aren't as tight, and we don't always have to be in a hurry. We are freer without a 5:30 A.M. wake-up call.

2) There is greater understanding and tolerance of yourself and others, and why folks act as they do.

3) Criticism is not earth shattering. You have come to grips with the fact that everyone is not going to like you, but that's okay. God will use someone else to reach them. You understand that "time wounds all heels." In addition, you accept the fact that you don't like everybody equally either!

4) There is less concern with finances as children are grown and educated. If I want a new dress I can buy it, and for once, not feel guilty.

5) The enjoyment of ordinary pleasures is heightened—lunch with a friend, an afternoon with a good book, an impromptu movie with your spouse.

6) There is freedom and flexibility to do things on the spur of the moment—no dogs to the vet, baby-sitters, or meal planning for those left at home.

7) You come to accept wrinkles, and looks do not seem to be as

important as when we were young. As Patsy Clairmont says, "Wrinkles are well-deserved grooves of maturity."

8) You've earned the right not to pretend or waste time with people or events that don't interest you. Time is of the essence and we want to spend it on things that fulfill.

Retirement Preparation

The next step for us will be retirement. I'm told this period of life can be like a river—either smooth sailing or white-water rafting, depending on how well we have planned ahead. According to the Alabama Mental Health Association, "Over 50 percent of Americans die in their first five years of retirement." However, you can avoid becoming part of this statistic. Only people who make proper preparation can face the future without fear or anxiety.

The thing that encourages me most about retirement is that the majority of our friends who have retired are happy. We have some good retirement role models, and I have made a practice of asking these what they consider to be the secret of their smooth adjustment. One whom I asked recently said the key was a prepared mind-set. I listened intently because not only was he retired himself, but during his career as a civilian personnel officer at a major air force base he counseled those facing voluntary or forced termination. Most large companies have preretirement counseling, and people should take advantage of that if it's available.

His observations regarding preparation included these three things:

1) If possible, work long enough to have adequate income to live without undue financial stress. Good advice for the young is, "Prepare for the years and not just the year." Someone said, "The one thing worse than dying is outliving your money."

2) Have something that you know from experience you enjoy doing. For him it was hunting, fishing, working in his shop, and involvement in building mission churches.

3) Don't fight it! This is a natural part of life's journey and one most everyone will eventually experience.

That is not to say this transition will be easy. In fact, I'm told the time of retirement puts a deep hurt in each of us. Psychologists rate that hurt as being half as traumatic as the loss of a lifelong mate. Serious adjustment is never easy, but "aging with grace" means never looking back. After all, we're not going in that direction! Every ounce of energy spent sulking over the past is energy that cannot be used surging toward the future.

Our big problem now is when and where—and these decisions are rarely simple! In fact, I've come to the conclusion that there are no easy decisions. My husband's answer to those who keep asking, "When?" is, "When it quits being fun!" Now, it has come close a time or two, but it is still fun! My answer to the "where?" is, "I'm waiting on the Lord to write it in the sky!"

I said that one day to a friend, and added, "I just can't seem to read His handwriting." Her response was, "It probably is not His handwriting but your eyesight!" I'm confident that is true, but I also believe His promise, "Behold, the former things have come to pass, and new things I declare: before they spring forth I tell you them" (Isa. 42:9).

Trusting the Lord does not mean you approach life unprepared. I'm doing everything I can and then trusting God to make good on His promises. Yes, growing old gracefully is no small feat, yet we must face the next periods of life with dignity, dreaming of journeys yet to come. God has been so good to us we are already living in a "bonus" situation.

Even the word "retirement" is harder to pin down these days. It used to be thought of as "the end of productivity." Now it's more likely to mean "the day on which you take your first pension check and move on to something new." Needless to say the first planning technique we need to engage in is probably to toss out the old rulebook! Whether we retire at sixty or seventy, we may easily have another twenty years of life.

There are those who believe that life begins at eighty. When my husband's mother was eighty she decided to write a book. Before she could do that she felt she needed to learn to type. She enrolled in a typing class at the YWCA, and then wrote her book. It was not a best seller, and only fifty to seventy-five copies were printed, but it was the story of their family—about how she and Landrum's dad met and married, with a chapter on each of the pastorates he served—and now it is one of our valued possessions. You know the will of God for your life. It is to keep on growing in grace and in the knowledge of our Lord and Savior Jesus Christ.

In July 1983 the number of Americans over 65 surpassed the number of teen-agers. More than two out of five who have passed 65 have passed 75. The fastest-growing age segment in our population is the 85+ group. When the twentieth century began there were only a few hundred thousand Americans over 85. Today there are 3.3 million, and it is estimated that by the year 2050 there will be 20 million. Have you noticed that Willard Scott has not run out of 100-year-olds to congratulate? There are estimated to be some 45,000 Americans over 100.

My point is that retirement age is no signal to mope around, just waiting for the funeral. There is life to be lived for all of us, and until God calls us home, let's live it to the fullest.

It is a mistake we mid-lifers make when we panic at the passing of our lives. I'm counting on our retirement to be not retiring from something, but retiring to some new activities. We shouldn't underestimate what the loss of a job means, but we shouldn't wallow in it, either. Too many people get stuck in that negative spiral, and retirees often become depressed, isolated, and bored. Accept reality—you are older and age takes its toll. You can't see as well, you can't hear as well, your memory is gone (C.R.S.—Can't Remember Squat!), you can't work as hard, but God didn't intend for each of us to have a thirty-year-old body throughout life, or He would have arranged it. But retiring from work should not be an excuse to retire from life. I have an optimistic friend who said to me, "I haven't retired, I have just relocated." I like that spirit!

Another good friend said, "We have always lived looking forward, and I anticipate the next day as the better one. Retirement is not an interruption in life unless people make it so. I remain ever grateful for health, the capacity to work, for the joy in the moments found with friends, and for life with its full cup."

Landrum and I were riding along in the car one day when he said in all seriousness, "Honey, do you think we are going to have enough to *do* when we retire?" I died laughing because having enough to do has never been our problem. However, quickly realizing he spoke in dead earnest, I said, "If you are healthy, you will be preaching, and besides, any Baptist church will keep you busy."

I do want to be sensitive, though, because I'm told a man's ego at retirement may be at its lowest point. Since men often define themselves by the work they do, retirement can feel like a loss of identity. If they have been forced to retire, they may be angry and bitter and filled with self-pity. Even if they have voluntarily retired, they may still feel subconsciously that they have been "put out to pasture."

Some husbands at loose ends begin to follow their wives around the house bossing them on how to cook, clean, and do those things they have done well for forty years. Or they may insist on going shopping with them. Now I think shopping for most women is a pleasant thing. If you happen to run into a friend in the aisle you may stop and visit for five or ten minutes. This is a "no-no" for most men. One friend suggested that a woman's great need:

> at the age of ten is for a playmate,
> at the age of twenty is for fun,
> at the age of thirty is for romance,
> at the age of forty is for fulfillment,
> at the age of fifty is for hard cash, and
> at the age of sixty is to be able to shop alone!

Like any major life change, retirement produces stress and requires adjustment. It is a loss, and we must recognize it as such. Just as there are stages usually experienced in a crisis, mental-health researchers have identified distinct stages in the retirement process. Bear in mind not everyone goes through these in the same order, but they can be a guide to what to expect.

1) *The Remote Stage.*
    This is much like the "deny" stage in a crisis. It is the refusal to think about retirement and to prepare for it.

2) *The Near Stage.*
    The inevitability of retirement dawns—it's coming "ready or not," and hopefully, we begin to plan for it.

3) *The "Honeymoon" Stage.*
    This has been described as the "euphoric" stage character-ized by thoughts like, "Finally, I can do what I want to do!"

4) *The Disenchantment Stage.*
    The "honeymoon" is over, and the initial excitement has

worn off. We are forced to face realities like loss of income, fewer activities, and that an important phase of our life is over.

5) *The Reorientation Stage.*
We must face the troubling aspects of retirement, and find a satisfying life-style. There can be surprising satisfaction in trying out new roles or exploring volunteer opportunities.

6) *The Stability Stage.*
The end result of disenchantment and reorientation should be a life-style of activities and routines that are comfortable and pleasing. Don't move from "womb" to "tomb" without making a ripple on the sea of life!

A danger facing all of us is that we will fall into verbal traps, which if repeated enough can be self-fulfilling prophecies and cause people to refer to us as a "mean old lady" or "crotchety old man." Let me tell you some.

1) When I was your age I used to . . .
2) I'm going to travel while I still have my health.
3) You can't teach an old dog new tricks.
4) When you get to be my age you'll understand.
5) I'm old enough to know better.
6) I'm going to take up golf while there's time.
7) It's too newfangled for me.
8) Well, I guess I'm good for another year.
9) At my age? Of course not.
10) I'm living on borrowed time.
11) Who wants to listen to an old duffer like me?
12) Life isn't what it used to be.
13) It's downhill from here on.
14) My get-up-and-go has got-up-and-went.

Completing the Journey

Our task is nothing more than completing the journey God has called us to do. The Christian pilgrimage is a moment-by-moment, daily journey. Each day is a part of a pilgrimage that prepares us for our eternal destiny. The old hymn says, "Then at last when on high

He sees us, our journey done, we will rest where the steps of Jesus end at His throne."

Neither you nor I can stop the aging process. Our skin grows older and more wrinkled. Our body begins to thicken and sag. We can slow down the process a bit by getting exercise, eating the right foods, and other methods, but not for long. We may even have to walk through life a bit slower and choose our steps more wisely, trusting a little more in Him who keeps us from stumbling.

Twentieth-century historians have characterized our generation as the "era of games and toys"—a preoccupation with earthly things. What we really need is to be "weaned from the temporal." He wants us to turn away from that which is deteriorating and to be "homesick for heaven"! Those who keep heaven in view can remain serene and cheerful on the darkest days.

What we so often forget is, life was not meant for gratification on earth, but for the development of a life for heaven. If the glories of heaven were more real to us, if we lived less for material things and more for things eternal and spiritual, we would be less easily disturbed by this present life. We would know that "Earth's best cannot bear comparison with heaven's least."

According to her daughter, when Mrs. Roland Leavell died in December 1974, among her belongings was found her Christmas list. Heading the list was the name *Lottie Moon*. The amount of money listed exceeded any other single gift. Mrs. Leavell's family and friends were not surprised. Throughout her life she always gave more to the Lottie Moon Offering for Foreign Missions than she gave to any other single person at Christmastime. It was her "Christmas gift to the Lord."

Only a few days before her death Mrs. Leavell was in charge of the Lottie Moon Day of Prayer at her church. She wrote members of her family to tell them about it. That letter arrived the same day relatives learned of her death.

Mrs. Leavell's letter said, "Being in charge of the Lottie Moon Day of Prayer was not too strenuous for me as some feared. But if it had been, it would have been a wonderful way to go to heaven."

Are you like me—you know what God has promised but you are still afraid of the unknown? We fear the approach of old age and its debilitating effects. It is the uncertain future that gives birth to doubts and fears. However, many of those things we fear never become reality—senility, loss of independence, confinement in a nursing home. Some interesting statistics about the 26 million adults over sixty-five are: 15 percent live with family; 80 percent live independent or semidependent lives; 5 percent live in nursing homes; 15 percent become senile. The good news is—85 percent of us will never become senile and 95 percent will never live in nursing homes! Scratch those worries and face the future triumphantly.

Faith is always oriented toward the future. "No mere man has ever seen, heard or even imagined what wonderful things God has ready for those who love the Lord" (1 Cor. 2:9 TLB).

The song says:

> One day Jesus will call my name.
> As days go by I hope I won't stay the same;
> I want to get so close to Him that it's no big change
> On the day that Jesus calls my name.

JOURNAL ENTRY

> "Fear not tomorrow; God is already there." Lord, help me to see Your hand in my life today, and trust the promise of Your presence with me tomorrow. When problems seem too big, let me simply do what I can and give the rest to You.

I wrote this chapter in the ICC unit of a Newnan, Georgia hospital where my brother-in-law is terminally ill with emphysema. Many have commented on his faith and the evident peace he has in the midst of his problems. The "fun and games" mentality won't cut it in testing times! Someone said, "Worship in the depth of sorrow is the test of perfect faith."

I read in my devotional book, and it is so true: "In that moment of facing death, everything looks so different! Wealth and fame, health and ambition—all these things previously so important, become insignificant in the scale of eternal values." When facing death, all things come into proper focus. As the old hymn says, "There are heights of joy that I may not reach/ Till I rest in peace with Thee."

Just remember that all healing is temporary. "There is a time to be born and a time to die." Don't worry about tomorrow. *The jour-*

ney is the joy. Make the most of the trip, even the bumpy places, knowing God is in control. All Christians are pilgrims moving toward our heavenly destination.

Think of:

> Stepping ashore and finding it heaven,
> of touching a hand and finding it God
> of breathing new air and finding it celestial
> of feeling invigorated and finding immortality
> of waking up and finding it home.

PRAYER

Lord, we do not know what the future holds, but help us know that heaven is eternity with You.

Into Your hands I lay the fears that haunt me,
The dread of future ills that may befall.
Into Your hands I lay the doubts that taunt me,
And rest securely, trusting You for all.

ALFRED O. CHRISTIANSEN

Questions for Chapter 11

1) What season of life are you living in now?
Spring—youthful life
Summer—carefree life
Fall—changing life
Winter—aging life
Are you making the most of this season of your life?

2) What do you believe are some advantages of aging?

3) Read 1 Cor. 2:9 and think about some of the wonderful things God has in store for you.

CHAPTER 12

Journey to Helpfulness

SOMEONE SAID, "THE ONLY CURE for suffering is to face it head on, grasp it around the neck, and *use* it!" This is what Joyce Landorf calls "a wounded healer" (Eph. 1:4 TLB). I guess the thing that has comforted me most during my crisis is my conviction that God could use my experience—that He never wastes *anything*. Regardless of what happens to us, we have the opportunity to make it sacred.

JOURNAL ENTRY

I'm praying that, whatever the reason for this experience, the Lord can use it later in His own timing for a testimony to His all sufficiency and care.

If we use our difficulties constructively, they can be a source of strength. We can *use* our pain rather than deny or avoid it. As Anita Bryant says, "We can take the garbage of our lives and turn it into compost."

JOURNAL ENTRY

I've just read about Joseph, Job, David, Paul, and Silas in situations life forced upon them. They responded far differently than I have. Forgive me for reacting in self-pity and frustration rather than responding with confidence in *You* and courage. Help me be an "overcomer." I read, "There is no pain, no suffering, no frustration, no disappointment that cannot be cured or taken up and used for higher ends."

I read the story a biologist told of watching an ant carry a piece of straw that was nearly too heavy to drag. The ant came to a crack in the ground that was too big to cross. Remaining still for a moment as though in deep concentration, the ant solved the problem. It pushed the straw over the crack and walked over on the straw. This is what Jesus did for us in salvation. He became the bridge between our sin and a righteous God, and this is what we can do by converting our burdens and sorrows into bridges that contribute to the well-being of others.

Trouble is truly universal. Sooner or later we will all see the wind (Matt. 14:22-31)! I think it was Elisabeth Elliott who said, "The more brokenhearted I became, the more understanding I was of the cry of other bleeding hearts, because I had tasted the cup of suffering."

Chuck Swindoll goes so far as to say that no one deserves the right to lead without first persevering through pain, heartache, and failure. He contends that those who are really worth following have paid their dues. You see, God gives us a ministry by first giving us a message—painful to learn, but precious to know and real to share. We resent these intruders, but our afflictions are the price we pay for our ability to sympathize. The Lord gives suffering so that we can help the suffering world.

Remember how many of David's psalms came out of his suffering, and without Paul's thorn we would have missed much of his tenderness. Through crushing experiences, the true perfume of life comes out. Look at Peter, who denied Christ. It was a terrible experience—yet when he got back on his feet, he blessed others. Perhaps we are being trained to be tutors for others when they hit the wilderness and the storms. The pressure of hard places helps us to understand the trials of others, and fits us to help and sympathize with them.

Jesus said, "What I tell you in darkness, that speak ye in light: and what ye hear in the ear, that preach ye upon the house tops" (Matt. 10:27). What does this mean to us? It means be quiet, listen to God when things are at their worst, and you will be able to talk to others when you are better. Those who come across your path need to know what you've learned. You have much to offer the world. God knows what it is, and He knows how to bring it out—to polish and refine it into blessing for others. Ron Dunn says, "God's gift to us becomes my responsibility to others."

JOURNAL ENTRY

Today I read, "When God wants to make a man, He puts him into a storm. Every man who is preeminent for his ability was first preeminent for suffering." The storms equip us for service—I would love to know what service You are equipping me for. You are preparing us through the trials of our lives at present for Your work "in the fullness of time."

I wrote the following letter to several friends who have experienced the whole gamut of human crises—cancer; loss of daughter or husband; miscarriage; rape. I wanted some firsthand information on what ministering act helped them the most.

Dear Pam,

I'm going to ask a favor and this is probably the last thing you are going to *want* to do. However, I think it might be *extremely* helpful to others who are going through a similar circumstance of facing cancer.

I'm writing a piece on "comforting others with the same comfort with which we have been comforted." Would you send me the ministering act that helped you the most in your illness, a copy of the notes (or several notes) that encouraged you the most, or any other kindness that saw you through those difficult days?

As I talk to those who have sorrowed, suffered, and hurt, usually they can point to one act of kindness that came at just the right moment for survival. It doesn't have to be in any perfect form, etc. (I'll edit it) if you will just write me the information. Okay?

Thanks a bunch.

Love,
Mrs. Landrum P. Leavell

I was interested to find that the very same things that helped me had blessed them. Next time you are in a quandary about what to say or do, begin with one of these suggestions.

Scripture Is a Must

Marge Caldwell said this Scripture held her up during the illness and death of her precious daughter, Gay: "For I know the plans I have for you," declares the Lord, "plans to prosper you and not to harm you, plans to give you hope and a future" (Jer. 29:11). Marge said:

> Yes! We have been brokenhearted! Yes! We've been painfully lonely for her! Yes! We've had days when we couldn't under-stand! Yes! We've cried and sobbed! Oh, yes! But through it all we've known Jesus' tremendous love—have felt His precious presence—we've healed through His Word—and Jer. 29:11 says it all! Beyond every valley of grief, there is a mountaintop of peace waiting for you!

When my daughter-in-law, Lisa, was hurting, a precious friend sent her a big brown envelope filled with biblical promises in indi-vidual white envelopes with these simple instructions: "Each day starting whenever you want to, pick one and only one envelope. Take it out of the big brown envelope, re-close the top, tear open the little white envelope and see what is awaiting you!"

I'm not talking about beating people over the head with Scriptures, but only One Who has suffered to the point of death and *conquered* is qualified to give both comfort and assurance.

Find Someone Who Understands

When we face our problems, we need the assurance that some-one who understands suffering is with us. A broken heart needs the ministry of another whose heart has been broken.

My friend Donna said when she found out her first pregnancy was ending in miscarriage, "I was devastated." Through the circum-stances of miscarriage she became acquainted with a neighbor who had just experienced the same thing and they became very close friends. She wrote:

> I think what ministered to me most was that she was there for me in all I went through because she knew the pain and

sorrow I was feeling and felt it with me. I try to do the same for anyone I know who is going through the hurt of a miscarriage. I've had several friends, and acquaintances who have "heard about me" and call me just to talk. I feel that by sharing with them and feeling what they feel helps to overcome a small portion of my hurt.

   The twenty-nine-year-old daughter of one of my dearest friends shared this with me about her bout with cancer:

   The thing that helped me through the last three years and still helps is women who have experienced the same thing I went through—mastectomies, chemotherapy and radiation—and have survived and are doing great. I guess the most exciting person I visited with was Ann Jillian. She called me at home after Nancy, my sister, had sent her a letter. She was very encouraging. Enclosed is a copy of a note and poem she sent me.

Dear Pam,

   Here is the prayer I live by every day that I promised in our conversation.

                    May God bless you always—
                    Ann Jillian

The same everlasting Father
Who cares for you today will take care of you
tomorrow and every day.
Either He will shield you from suffering,
or He will give you unfailing strength to bear it.
Be at peace then and put aside
all anxious thoughts and imaginings.

                    ST. FRANCIS DE SALES

   This is the article that appeared in the newspaper describing Ann's call to Pam:

Actress Encourages Cancer Sufferer

It would seem that the best person to help a woman through the trauma of breast cancer would be another woman who had the experience. It is even more comforting when the other woman is a famous actress who has returned to her career full force, according to Pam Vann, a Wichita Falls cancer patient.

Vann received a surprise phone call Thursday night from actress Ann Jillian, whose struggle with breast cancer and subsequent mastectomy has been widely publicized and was the subject of a television movie.

"The call was such a shock," Vann said. "She's such a nice person to visit with. She was very encouraging and easy to talk with."

Vann, who is married and has two small children, underwent a mastectomy last November at the age of 29.

"I have a family history so I was cautious," she said. "But you don't expect it when you're so young."

Vann's sister had written a letter to Jillian via *Redbook* magazine. Her sister thought Jillian could be a source of comfort to her, Vann said, because, although family and friends are sympathetic, the actress had actually experienced breast cancer.

"I still kind of pinch myself," Vann said. "She was very concerned, very positive."

She said that what she most remembers about the 20-minute conversation was Jillian emphasizing that Vann was not alone in her battle with the disease. "She said there are many women who go through this and are able to lead productive and wonderful lives," Vann recalled. "They appreciate the time, and every day is special. She made it seem like I'm not the only one."

Vann has finished chemotherapy treatments and is halfway through the radiation therapy. She said she "feels great" and is regaining her strength, and the pep talk from Jillian definitely helped. "She was a real inspiration," she said.

We asked our good friend who is a dentist why he wasn't going to a dental convention being held in a nearby city. His reply was, "I have been to my last convention to listen to a 'dry finger' dentist." It just proves once again that those who lack experience in a given area have little to say to those going through the daily problems. In others words, don't tell me how to do it if you haven't done it!

Share Something Tangible

When tragedy strikes someone you know, it is important to acknowledge the event and his or her pain. The best way for me to do this is with a personal note. Maybe this is a "chicken" way, but I would much rather write her *before* I run into her in the grocery store or at church. A friend calls these, "God's little love notes."

These little notes are also great healers for family members. Lan left notes all over the house when he visited following my "episode." I came to refer to them as "phantom notes" because I don't know how he found all those places. He even wrote in my journal, and *nobody* sees my journal!

It was weeks before I found them all, and guess what? They are still there. Even though they are dingy and the edges have curled up, they give me a nice warm feeling every time I see one reminding me of his love. It is amazing what encouraging thoughts on scraps of paper can do for one in the "valley."

Most people in the throes of a trauma have time on their hands. I found it extremely comforting when a friend of mine sent quotes, Scriptures, or prayers on a regular basis with a note that simply said, "These have helped me when I hurt." Ann Jillian's poem is a good example.

I heard someone this very week mention "Casserole Christians." I love it! Many who feel they never know what to "say" often express their love and concern with a casserole. My husband probably would have *starved* when I could barely function had it not been for "Casserole Christians."

One of my former student wives was in deep despair following the death of her young husband by suicide. She said one of the most thoughtful gestures she remembers was a neighbor who offered to cut her grass. It bears out the truth of the old song that says, "Little things mean a lot."

I remember reading a testimony from another young widow left with two boys approaching their teen-age years. She said the Lord provided numerous male role models for her sons. A second cousin picked up the boys Tuesday and Thursday mornings and took them to school. Another friend called when the Magic Johnson story broke, offering to explain to the boys what Magic meant when he said he was retiring because he was HIV-positive. Now, that is a *real* friend!

Your Presence Is the Best Gift of All

Ask any hurting person if he or she would rather have pills or people, and I guarantee you most will say, "People." There is no substitute for *a warm body*. Loneliness is the most devastating malady there is.

One man, speaking of the death of his wife, told of his loneliness. He said he tried to stay busy and keep his mind off himself, but he couldn't avoid the empty chair at the table or the empty bed and the accompanying silence. He told of the things he tried to do to compensate, such as eating out when he couldn't afford it, just to be with people. He found opportunities to go into stores. People at church prayed for him and asked God to help him with his loneliness, but no one yet invited him to spend the evening with them.

How often have I prayed for God to relieve a person's loneliness or illness when what He really wants is to strengthen and encourage that one through me? I'll ever be grateful to Becky Brown, who spent the nights at our house when Landrum was out of town. She came late and left early, but oh, how it helped just to have someone "there."

JOURNAL ENTRY

I am *so* grateful not to be alone while feeling like I do. Becky is spending the nights with me, and that is a comfort. She took me to Camellia Grill last night and to Sam's Wholesale Club, which was a change and did me good. If I just knew where the medical ends and the nerves begin I could better handle my weird feelings. Lord, please give me *peace!*

Lisa, my daughter-in-law, had the same offer from a friend: "If Roland is out of town, there is room at our house for you. You are special and I want you to feel safe." She also had another thoughtful friend who wrote, "If you need someone to listen—or if you need someone to jabber away about nonsense just to take your mind off things—I'm here. I'll admit that my special talent lies in the latter, but I'm not a bad listener when it gets right down to it."

Donna wrote this about her miscarriage night:

> Jeff and I were very scared. Amy and Ken were *there for us*. They went with us to the hospital and Amy stayed with me the entire time in the emergency room until I was moved to a room. After I came home, when the surgery had been done, she was still *there for me*.

The key words are *there for me*. Why are we so uncomfortable with the griefstricken? Often we hesitate to contact a hurting family because we think we have to have answers for them or we think we'll say or do the wrong thing. So, instead of moving toward people in need, we tend to pull away or avoid them. It matters little what you "say"; the important thing is simply to be there.

I never will forget when my first child was born. Lan was delivered a month early by Caesarean section because of my high blood pressure problems. I had virtually *no* experience around babies, he was little, and I was *scared*. My sweet mother came, stayed in the hospital room with me because there was no nursery in the small country hospital where he was born, and took good care of me and my baby. At the end of two weeks it became necessary for her to return home. I always said about the morning she left, "I don't know who cried more—Lan or me!"

The first evening I was alone a practical nurse in our church came to visit. As she left she asked, "Would you like me to come in the morning and bathe the baby?" I can't tell you the relief I felt. She came, and even offered to come the second day. However, in her wisdom on that day she asked, "Why don't you bathe Lan and I'll be right here beside you if you need help?" It is hard to believe after all my experience now with babies and grandbabies that I was ever that afraid, but I was. That friend gave me the confidence I needed as she came "alongside for a season."

Don't Place Blame or Guilt

Some of our problems are self-inflicted—tensions of our own

making; some result from outward circumstances and pressures beyond our control; and many have absolutely no explanation. It is a lesson in futility to try to "explain" everything. One friend, suffering because of her parents' divorce, said she received great comfort when her brother-in-law assured her, "Remember that we love you and we don't condemn you or your parents." Grieving people need to know that we aren't judging them, and that we don't have a timetable for when they should be "over this."

Remember the Value of Touch

The first act of the risen Savior was to place His right hand on John. Jesus often touched people to comfort them. His touch communicated both His blessing and His power. Someone said, "God gave you arms, just the right size, for reaching around your brothers and sisters." When Jesus wants to give somebody a hug, He has to use *your* arms.

I'll never forget the morning in Baton Rouge when Ginny placed her hand on my shoulder and said, "Let's pray." It had the most calming effect on me, much like a nice warm blanket of love.

God taught us much about touch through Jesus. He walked across Israel, extending His hand and heart, and touching any who needed His healing touch. He called children to Himself; He touched a blind man's eyes and restored his sight; He touched a deaf man's ears and made him hear again.

Jesus reached out and touched others, and others reciprocated and touched Jesus. A sick woman touched Jesus' garment and was instantly healed; a prostitute reached out and touched Jesus' feet, bathed them in expensive perfume, and wiped them with her hair; a rich man reached out to Jesus and gave Him a tomb from which to come forth alive!

Look for someone who needs a physical or emotional hug today. It is when we exercise "high touch," allowing others to reach out to us, that we come in contact with a magnificent mystery called relationship. It often begins with a single encounter. Don't turn away from even the smallest impulse that motivates you. Such an encounter may hold a giant amount of *joy* for someone else. Pray, "Lord, help me see a needy life and a challenge that is just my size."

The outcome of our "journey inward" is a "journey outward" to meet the needs of the world. We are able to give to others the compassion we received. Work on your relationships. It's "pay-back time." Do something helpful for another person at least once a week. Many people with long-term illnesses tell how they get cards and calls in the first few days or weeks of their sickness. But too soon the mailbox is empty, the phone silent, and the visitors dwindle. Norman Vincent Peale suggests we ask the Lord to put someone in our path before sundown who is discouraged—someone downhearted who needs a lift and isn't expecting to get one. Ask the Lord, further, to help you recognize such a person when you encounter one. If you ask Him to send you one person you can help, He is likely to send you a dozen.

Focusing on others teaches us to be less selfish and less preoccupied with our own problems. If we have our eyes upon ourselves, our problems, and our pain, we cannot lift our eyes upward. A child looks up when he's walking with his father, and the same should be true for the Christian. "I lift up my eyes to the hills—where does my help come from? My help comes from the Lord, the Maker of heaven and earth" (Ps. 121:1-2 NIV®). It is the meaninglessness of suffering which destroys. If we can find meaning and significance to what is happening to us and give out of our weakness and from our heart, that engenders *joy*.

PRAYER

May the suffering of my life be used to comfort others and to glorify our Heavenly Father. Help me whenever, wherever, and however I can to bring light to someone who sits in darkness.

Questions for Chapter 12

1) What Scriptures have most ministered to you during a time of crisis?

2) How have Christian friends or family ministered to you in a time of need? List their acts of kindness below and thank God for them.

3) Read these Scriptures about Jesus touching others: Matt. 20:29-34, Mark 1:40-42, Luke 22:50-51. Have you allowed Jesus to use your touch to help those who are hurting?

CHAPTER 13

Responsibilities of the Upward Journey

ISN'T IT AMAZING how the Lord will impress upon our hearts one little phrase from the wealth of material that enters our minds on any given day? Two such phrases are we need to "praise Jesus," and we need to "use Jesus." Let's consider the first of these.

Praise Jesus

I. *Praise Him—*

"Sickness teaches us that activity is not the only way to serve God," says Billy Graham in his book *Hope for the Troubled Heart.* I'm so glad. You see, an illness can start you on a spiritual journey of prayer and praise that will be richer than anything you ever dreamed possible.

When we gaze at Jesus and praise Him, we are much more able to just glance at our circumstances that are so difficult. As we gaze, we advance and are slowly being changed into His likeness.

"Praise" can also be translated as "bless." We bless, praise, and thank the Lord for Who He is and for all He has done for us. Does your praise concentrate more on what He has done than on Him?

JOURNAL ENTRY

Today, Lord, I don't want a thing. I just want to love You!

I can safely say no one can know what praise and thanksgiving are until you have come out of a wilderness experience. When you have clung to Him through pain and problems and experienced His *amazing grace,* you find *joy* in *Him.*

One of our best-known hymns and a favorite of many Christians is "Amazing Grace." John Newton wrote this hymn in 1779. Most of us can sing at least the first and last stanzas from memory. The first verse emphasizes the grace of God at the time of our salvation experience. The last verse underscores our praising God throughout eternity for His grace.

The third verse, however, may not be as familiar to some: "Thro' many dangers, toils, and snares, I have already come; 'Tis grace has bro't me safe thus far, and grace will lead me home." Can you think of a better reason for praise?

I watched the 1993 presidential inauguration and marveled again at the acclaim we give earthly leaders. Rightly so—but how much more should we bow before the King of Kings and Lord of Lords. Scripture tells us the "elders fell down before the Lamb" (Rev. 5:8), and even Paul said, "I bow my knees unto the Father of our Lord Jesus Christ" (Eph. 3:14).

I remember when I was in high school spending many nights with one of my good friends. Her mother was a widow raising three children alone. When we came in from the movie or a party we passed her room on our way to bed. Through a crack in the door I often saw her on her knees by the bed praying. The picture in my mind of that scene still blesses me. How fortunate children are to be brought up in such a home.

Worship flows from a grateful heart as a natural response to God's gracious revelation of Himself. In speaking of our relationship to God, the Bible says far more about joy than it does about duty. It urges people to be joyful in their worship, and it promises that their lives will be joyful because of their worship. Public praise of the Savior is important for all believers even if our worship styles differ. Under whatever form, worship expresses gratitude, love, and praise to God for His goodness and grace.

The Psalms came to mean so much to me since my illness. I have always loved the Psalms, but I have read them with new insight. It has been an immense blessing. Ps. 84:1-2 says, "How amiable are thy tabernacles, Oh, Lord of Host! My soul longeth, yea, even fainteth for the courts of the Lord: my heart and my flesh crieth out for the living God."

The Psalmist evidently for some reason had been denied access to the temple. It wasn't as if there were a temple on every corner as churches are now. People had to travel a great distance to the temple in many cases. Perhaps the Psalmist had been unable to go for worship because of illness. The Scripture says, "My soul longeth, yea, even fainteth for the courts of the Lord."

Wouldn't it be wonderful if we felt like that about worship? I don't know why it is that some people *long* to be in the house of God while others take it for granted. I have always loved church. Maybe it was because I grew up in a nominal Christian home where my parents went on Sunday morning and that was the extent of their churchgoing. You don't have to make me go to church. That was true even in my teen-age years. I have always *loved* being in the house of God.

Never forget the admonition in Ps. 145:4: "One generation shall praise thy works to another, and shall declare thy mighty acts." Pass on the praise to your children and grandchildren.

JOURNAL ENTRY

I get so excited when I feel that a passage of Scripture speaks directly to me. Ps. 145:1-7 did that for me this morning—*pass on the praise.* Help me to be faithful in that—I had a wonderful example in Annie. She always praised the Lord to her children.

Praise Him for His blessings. "I will praise Thee, O Lord, with my whole heart; I will shew forth all Thy marvelous works" (Ps. 9:1). Anita Bryant says:

Go home and begin to list every good gift God has given you. *Everything.* List your gifts carefully and fully, then offer them back to God!

If you want a memorable worship experience, just begin to recall times when God blessed your life in a special way. Think and thank Him for the gift of life and for His providential care. Thank Him for the gifts that make that life good, and for the gift of eternal life. Praise Him for every blessing you can remember.

Gratitude should characterize us now—before we lose the abundance lavished on us. *Never forget* Ps. 106:7 and 21. The Israelites "forgot" their Savior and the great things that had been done in

Egypt. What if tomorrow's supply depended on today's thanksgiving? Praise Him regardless of the content of the day. A good healthy dose of praise and thanksgiving will cure many an ill.

Praise Him for the thorns. Praise does not stop when the clouds come. Active faith will praise God in the darkest night. Someone said, "Christians *praise* when 'feeling good.' If we praise God 'on the mountaintop' but refuse to praise Him 'in the valley,' we are praising our feelings."

JOURNAL ENTRY

George Matheson (blind preacher of Scotland) said, "My God, I have never thanked Thee for my thorn. Teach me the value of my thorn." We forget that our hard situation may be the very condition of our blessing. My continued stress is a constant reminder of my weakness and dependence upon thee. ". . . For when I am weak, then am I strong" (2 Cor. 12:10). Literal translation is: "Therefore I take pleasure in being without strength . . . for when I am without strength, then am I dynamite."

As we move on through Ps. 84 we come upon problems in verses 6-7a. "Who passing through the valley of Baca make it a well; the rain also filleth the pools. They go from strength to strength. . . ."

What was the valley of Baca? I'm told the word comes from a verb that means "to weep." This has often been thought of as a waterless, barren valley through which the pilgrims passed on their way to Jerusalem. Because of their faith, they turned it into a spring. The lesson for us is, we are going to have some colorless walks. We are going to pass through some barren valleys on this journey called life. However, our attitude toward these problems can turn them into a learning, joyful experience.

All *things* are *not* good, but the promise from God is *He* works all things together for *good*. I never thought any good could come out of my recent experiences, but I will have to tell you it has. You think you are going under when those valley experiences come, but God walks with us through those bad times and as we trust in Him, He can turn those experiences into a spring of blessing. These people had a resilient attitude, because of their desire to worship Him, and were willing to go through hardships. They were

not going to be put down and discouraged because of those hardships. I have been told that "choosing our attitude is ultimate freedom." Yes, there are problems in every walk of life, but we can
choose our response to them.

We seldom grow on the mountain but rather in the valley. Under
pressure is where we learn the secrets of God. Comfort and prosperity have never enriched us like adversity. "The silences of Jesus
are as eloquent as His speech. . . . Thou shalt yet *praise* Him, yes,
even for His silence."

II. *Pray to Him—*

When life is out of control, prayer sounds like a weak alternative,
but in reality is the highest work of a believer. In the midst of problems and difficulties, our genuine faith will be expressed by earnest
prayer, which enables us to know the presence of God on the journey of life.

I had an experience that gave me a new way of looking at the
power of prayer. Following my dad's death, my mother moved to
Brunswick, Georgia to be near my oldest sister. Her home was situ-
ated on an acre lot surrounded by trees, shrubs, and grass, which
required constant maintenance. She loved yard work, but with the
passage of time, cutting the lawn became quite a chore for her.
Each time we went to visit, Landrum, all our children, and I would
give what assistance we could. I will long remember one morning
when I went out to cut the grass. I can safely say that I have *never*
worked any harder than I did pushing the mower that day. When I
came in for a break, I asked my mother how in the world she was
able to mow the grass when I, who was almost forty years younger,
was having such a hard time. Landrum overheard our conversation, and went out to investigate the problem. I was astounded as
he flipped a small lever and began following the mower. Can you
imagine my chagrin when I realized I had been pushing a self-pro-
pelled lawn mower?!

I recently related that story to a friend, and we had a good laugh
at my naïveté. Then my friend became serious and asked, "Isn't
that the way we Christians do when we attempt to live our lives
without the benefit of the Holy Spirit's power?"

I have since thought about the many problems and situations I
have "pushed" in my life. Why is it we insist on doing things in our

puny strength when His power is readily available with the flip of a lever called prayer?

Prayer is the pause that empowers. Just because the situation is desperate does not mean that we are. As long as I hold on to God in prayer, I'm going to be safe in my spiritual journey. To *walk* with God we must make it a practice to *talk* with God.

Prayer is not so much getting things from God as it is getting God's viewpoint about things. It is submitting to God, not using God. It is seeking God's will rather than demanding my own. It is not "Gimme, gimme, gimme," but "Lord, what will you have me do?"

Prayer is as much listening to God as it is talking to God. It is dialogue, not monologue.

Prayer is spending time with God for His own sake—not just asking and running. Prayer's preoccupation is the glory of God's name, the coming of God's kingdom, the doing of God's will.

True prayer is simply to know God! Prayer may not change things, but may change you for things.

III. *Sing to Him—*

"Therefore, the redeemed of the Lord shall return, and come with singing unto Zion; and everlasting *joy* shall be upon their head: they shall obtain *gladness* and *joy*; and sorrow and mourning shall flee away" (Isa. 51:11). That verse tells me that singing and sighing do not coexist. Blessed beyond measure is the Christian who can sing the Lord's songs in the darkest night. I found it to be one of the quickest ways to move from doubt to faith. Doubts come, questions rise, but the Good Shepherd walks before us to lead, guide, and guard His own *through* the valley—with the emphasis on the *through*. That's His promise in Ps. 23.

Probably the two best known songs of praise in the Bible are from the lips of two women—Hannah and Mary. You remember that Hannah had no children and prayed earnestly for a baby. According to Scripture, she poured out her soul before the Lord (1 Sam. 1:15), and "her countenance was no more sad" (verse 18).

When the angel announced to Mary that she would be the mother of the Son of God, she spoke those immortal words: "For with God nothing shall be impossible. . . . Be it unto me according to Thy word" (Luke 1:37-38). Then she broke into a song of praise known by Christians all over the world:

> And Mary said, "My soul doth magnify the Lord,
> And my spirit hath rejoiced in God my Savior.
> For He hath regarded the low estate of His handmaiden:
> For behold, from henceforth all generations shall call me blessed.
> For He that is mighty hath done to me great things;
> And holy is His name" (Luke 1:46-49).

The interesting thing about both of these women is that rejoicing came with the act of submission *before* they knew the end result of their prayers. That says to me, praise *is* possible even during the darkest nights.

It appears the deepest songs are not sung during life's richest blessings, but when we become aware of being a part of God's plan, which is bigger than our agendas.

Life is far more tragic than orderly, and seldom lends itself to what Larry Crabb calls "recipe theology." Formulas always fail. I'm convinced the answers to our problems are not found in "five easy steps" or "four principles of this or that." The most important issues of life never operate on a formula mentality, so don't look at problems as something to be solved but as chances to know God better. He is the only One Who can give us a song in the darkest night.

Even though my husband is a minister, I will have to tell you that during this time, music comforted me more than preaching. The words from old hymns took on new meaning. So often we sing without ever engaging our minds. I will never forget a duet sung on Sunday, February 24, 1991, with these words:

> God is too wise to be mistaken.
> God is too good to be unkind.
> When you don't understand,
> When you don't see His plan,
> When you can't trace His hand,
> Trust His heart.

There are many things you are not going to understand, but "God gives a song through the night season as all the day long."

JOURNAL ENTRY

> I will thank and *praise* Thee for this puzzle, and trust where I cannot understand. I rejoice to be counted worthy of this testing. Help me to cling more tightly to Your guiding hand.

How long has it been since you let yourself savor the pure joy of listening to music—not the songs on the radio, crowded in as you speed along the highway—but actually bathed yourself in the music you love most? Someone said comfort came to him most from Scripture, friends, and old hymns.

We were in Columbus, Mississippi one weekend, and the pastor there offered to let me use his office during the early service. I planned to be in the eleven o'clock service, but wanted some quiet time for study. He said, "Do you like Dino?" I responded that I did so he put a tape in of instrumental music—no words, just music. That was the most soothing time, and *gladness* and *joy* did come and sighing fled away!

"I will sing unto the Lord as long as I live: I will sing praise to my God while I have my being" (Ps. 104:33).

Once I had this note from a precious friend after I had given my testimony:

> Dear Jo Ann,
>
> I can relate so well to your turning to music when you thought God was not hearing your prayers. I have gotten to the point where I require little sleep because pain keeps me awake most of the night. I put my bedside radio on one night on 89.1 (Christian music) and now it plays every night, all night.
>
> God has spoken to me more in listening to music in the middle of the night than any amount of praying I could do. And you know I believe He is there with me. I can feel His presence. It's almost as if He were saying, "Marilyn, listen to the words of this song," and I fall into a restful and peaceful sleep for a while.
>
> How good Jesus is to me during the long nights when no one else in the world knows what's going on inside of me. He *do,* He do!!!

Keep listening to your music, Jo Ann, there is untold comfort in it. I can even sing along now. I'll be thinking of you and hoping that you are singing along with me.

God has many sharp cutting instruments and rough files for the polishing of His jewels; and those He especially loves and means to make the most resplendent, He uses His tools on often. Let's pray we're in that number.

Lovingly, Marilyn

Music is just one of the ways we can praise God, but I have found it to be one of the best.

What is the place of music in your spiritual life? Can you use the word "joy" to describe your experience with the Lord? If not, pray as David prayed: "Restore unto me the joy of my salvation." Pray with another: "Great Master, touch us with Thy skillful hands and let not the music that is in us die!" Thank God for the great music that helps us worship and praise.

James says:

Is anyone among you suffering? Let him pray. Is anyone cheerful? Let him sing praises (James 5:13 NAS).

The truth is that everyone suffers somewhere along life's journey. Life will never be painless. Stress seems to be at epidemic levels today. How many times have you read articles or heard TV reports about stress in the home and marketplace? It is a fact that we are all suffering and grabbing for handles to cope with the challenges that life brings our way.

James' first suggestion is easy—pray when suffering. Most of us instinctively pray in times of trouble, and when we are cheerful it is easy to sing. Singing joyous praises for blessings is another form of prayer. What better way to pray concerning our joy than to "sing songs of praises"? The really tough part is to sing when suffering!

There are several things we can count on in this life.

1) *Storms are inevitable.* These are the times that "try" our faith. These are the moments when we are most aware of our dependence upon God.

JOURNAL ENTRY

My faith continues to be weak when it concerns my health. I don't understand that because I seem to be able to *trust* in every other area. I'm sure it is because I've come to the end of my strength and what I can do. I know God is teaching me and keeping away encouraging results until I learn this lesson. It's the hardest test I have ever had.

Storms may vary and we need to be aware of individual differences. Someone reminded me that what is a storm to one person may just be a shower to someone else, and that we have no right to downgrade someone else's hurricane to a tropical storm. I think I've learned that lesson *well.*

JOURNAL ENTRY

Rain, rain, rain! We are experiencing a thunderstorm right now—I feel as if that is the way my life has been for months now—cloudy, dark, not good. I know the sun *will* shine again, but it is so hard to hang on to that right now. Yesterday was *not* a good day—I *praise* you for being with me even in the cloudy days!

2) *God is bigger than any storm He allows.* What do you do when things are bad and look as if they are going to get worse? Paul and Silas "prayed, and sang praises unto God," *and* I might add that they were even in jail. Believe me, God is the *only* One Who does not change with changing circumstances. He is dependable no matter what. "Praise the Lord, He never changes." God knows what He is doing.

3) *Expressing faith in God helps us.* You may ask, "How can I sing when I am afraid and my heart is heavy?" All I know is, many of the Psalms moved from desperate pleas for help to praise. All but Ps. 88 have some note of praise in them. God is worthy of praise whatever the circumstances. Praise helps pass time and chase away panic.

Use Jesus

When I first came across the idea of "using" Jesus, I was literally repulsed at the idea. It sounded so manipulative and arrogant. Then I realized the sense in which it was being used: that of total dependence on His power for ministry. As we journey through life, we must move from the place of praise and prayer to a place of ministry. We rise from authentic prayer with eyes open to see the opportunities for ministry in Christ's name. Worship and works cannot be separated.

Can a person possess saving faith without demonstrating that faith in service? That question has been asked for generations, but the Bible teaches a dynamic relationship between saving faith, standing faith, *and* serving faith. The result of saving faith will be seen. Dr. Herschel Hobbs says, "The next greatest tragedy to a lost soul is a saved soul and a lost Christian life." Yes, we are saved by grace through faith, but saving faith moves us to a life-style of service. We can't separate salvation from a call to service. Christians and most pagans recognize the close association that should exist between belief and behavior. We are saved to serve, not sit—verifying our faith.

James reminds us of this in 2:14: "What good is it, my brothers, if a man claims to have faith but has no deeds? Can such faith save him?" (NIV®). This word *deeds* is translated in other places *action,* reminding us that faith without action is both shallow and empty. Serving faith gives evidence that we have saving faith.

I've always had a hard time with people who don't put feet to their prayers. It is easy to say, "I'll pray for you," but it takes time, courage, and compassion to get involved in the lives of others.

The reason why many people feel that the Christian life is dull and drab is because they have never progressed from saving faith to serving faith. Serving faith is exciting and gives vitality to our lives. It exchanges spiritual emptiness and resignation for celebration and risk-taking obedience.

Faith should be a verb that expresses itself in our actions. If that is true, why is it so few are willing to turn faith into Christian energy? Why do we avoid ministry? I believe we are just too busy to help the needy. We are wrapped up in our selfish life-styles and so "programmed" that we, like the priest and Levites in the biblical account of the story of the good Samaritan, just pass by on the other side.

What was the good Samaritan doing on that road? He was

"passing through" from Jerusalem to Jericho. Much of our lives is spent "passing through." Do you recall the song we used to sing, "This world is not my home; I am just 'passing through'"? Another says:

> While passing thro' this world of sin,
> Others your life shall view.
> Be clean and pure without, within.
> Let others see Jesus in you.

Often when we see Jesus in Scripture, He was "passing through." He was talking by the side of the well, healing physical difficulties, and debating with the Pharisees. When it is all said and done, "passing through" is all we are doing. I don't care what age you are, you are not going to be here long. What is your attitude while "passing through"? What do other people gain from your presence? How do you measure up to opportunities that present themselves along the way?

Phillips Brooks was a great preacher in New England. It was said in the newspaper about him, "Yesterday opened cloudy and unpleasant. But about noon Phillips Brooks came downtown, and everything brightened up." Have you been around people who made you feel good to be around them? What an influence. When you walk through the streets does it help? Do others get a lift from your presence? What about your family? Sometimes we can be nicer to others than we are to those who live under our own roof.

Some have called Ps. 101 David's inauguration speech. It is a psalm of "I shalts" and "I wills." One of those is, "I will walk *within my house* . . ." (verse 2). That is the determination that ought to characterize your life and mine. If there is anything I want to be it is an *authentic* Christian. I want to be the same yesterday, today, and forever. I want to be above-board with nothing to hide. We use the expression, "What you see is what you get." This is the way I want to live, and I want to be the same at home as I am at church. It's hard. I'm not saying it is easy, but our first duty is to those in our home. Are you a saint abroad, and a devil at home? What we are at home is who we are indeed!

People everywhere are hurting for a variety of reasons. They may be lonely, sick, involved in a painful marriage or divorce, sorrowing over the loss of a child or mate, or living with uncertainty as I was. Many others are without Christ and without hope—spiritually lost.

Often a crisis provides an open door to the gospel. Witnessing to some people may be a dead-end street, until they are sick, hospitalized, unemployed, or grieving. Love people in their crisis times, and maybe you can introduce them to Jesus.

Often we earn the right to share our convictions by first sharing our difficulties. When we can identify with others' hurts, they are more open to an explanation of what gives you strength and what Jesus means to you. I'm convinced nobody comes through your life by accident. Christians are planted in places to be fruitful.

When we are honest, a surprised world will give a second thought to the possibility that Christ can make a difference in a man or woman's life. It becomes a challenge to find that point of need in a person's life. You will begin to see hurt in people's eyes and maybe in the way their shoulders slump. Watch for it.

The aging segment in our society is growing by leaps and bounds. It has been called "the graying of America." Understanding their needs and trying to meet them is an investment in others, and the personal touch is indispensable. There is no substitute for caring hands reaching out. "The way from God to a human heart is through a human heart" (S. D. Gordon). A good prescription may be: prepare with prayer; dare to share; follow up with care.

I have made a new commitment not to ignore the suffering and pain of hurting people, but to act redemptively on behalf of others. What about you? Who knows—the next one to suffer just may be *you!* Herschel Hobbs reminds us: "If you have a cup of cold water in your hand, give it to someone who is thirsty."

God gives us a ministry by first giving us a message. No one deserves the right to be heard without persevering through pain, heartache, and failure. However, once we have a message, we must actively reach out. Blessings should flow through you, not just to you!

The use of the word *abundance* in Matt. 25:29 describes the blessings God pours on us for our trust in Him. Whatever we commit to Him will be returned with interest, according to this parable of the talents. The five-talent person and the two-talent person, if faithful, are told the same thing: "Well done, good and faithful servant. Enter thou into the joy of the Lord!"

JOURNAL ENTRY

> I've always wanted *boldness* in witnessing. Marsha Spradlin wrote that after her extended illness "the fear of sharing my faith was gone." Oh, that would be true!! I read today about Peter and John having boldness in witnessing. The people marveled and took note they "had been with Jesus." I'm sure that is how boldness comes. During this holding pattern, this divine waiting on You as the Great Physician, refine me that I can be a bolder witness.

How is it with you? Is your relationship with the Lord so vital that you want to share all He has done? Can you say with the Psalmist, "I have put my trust in the Lord God, that I may declare all thy works"? Our job is to "pass it on"—to leave something worthwhile behind.

JOURNAL ENTRY

> My class is tonight, and this statement was such an encouragement to me—"We are doing more good than we know, sowing seed, starting streamlets, giving men true thoughts of Christ, to which they will refer one day as the first things that started them thinking of Him."

Ministering is for believers, not just for people in ministry. I'm told that 50 percent of people will respond to the call of Christ if asked. There are people out there ready, just waiting for you and me. The fields truly are ripe unto harvest. I pray daily that I can be the spark to ignite others!

I want to leave you with three *B* words. The first one is *brevity*. You don't have long to make your mark. The song says, "Time is now fleeting; the moments are passing." You may be a young married person but, believe me, it is a short ride. I cannot believe I am in my sixties. There is no way I could be convinced without my birth certificate. Life is brief and anything I plan to do, I had better get at it.

My daughter and her husband served a church in Baton Rouge for ten years. One of their faithful members retired, bought an expensive motor home, and planned to travel. He told a friend who went with him to get gas, "I figure I've got ten good years left to travel." They got the gas, went back home, and he had a heart attack and died getting out of that motor home. You say, "Jo Ann, that is a scare tactic." No! It can happen. We have no guarantee we are going to be here tomorrow. We have no guarantee we have one, ten, or fifteen years left. Whatever we plan to do, we better get at it because life is brief.

The second *B* is *blessing*. There are many who never get in the action enough to be blessed. If we don't *do something,* we are not going to make any contribution. Jesus said, "Well done, good and faithful servant"—*not* well intentioned but *well done!* Don't miss the blessing of making a difference as you "pass through."

I am told in witnessing that people are much more responsive if you have *any* sort of personal relationship with them. Every one of us has at least twelve people we know on a first-name basis who need the Lord or the ministry of our church. What about your beauty operator, grocery clerk, teachers, office workers? Don't miss the blessing of being a witness to them.

The third *B* is *bequest*. That usually has to do with something given to someone else, usually in a will. What we leave, we bequeath to others. It is passed on. I'm using it in this sense.

When our first Leavell grandson was born, Lisa, his mother, designed his birth announcement. She had the cleverest idea. He is named Roland Q. Leavell III for his father, Roland Q. Leavell II. My son was not a junior because he was named for his great-uncle, Dr. Roland Q. Leavell. Lisa had the idea for the front of the announcement to have three stick figures. She had secured a picture of Dr. Roland Q. Leavell, of my son, Roland, and a newborn picture of baby Ro. She used the theme from the Olympics of carrying the torch. When that announcement came, I nearly folded, but isn't that what life is all about? We are passing the torch from one generation to another.

We have seen this in the remarkable Leavell family as generation after generation have served the Lord faithfully. We have also seen the opposite truth portrayed, which proves the statement that you can go from Christianity to paganism in one generation. We have

212 JOY IN THE JOURNEY

seen children of missionary parents become inactive and grandchildren who do not even know the Lord. If we don't pass the
torch and influence the next generation, chances are it won't be
done. Get serious about training your replacement! Success without a successor is failure.

James Dobson has suggested that this mission can be likened to
a three-man relay race:

> First, your father runs his lap around the track, carrying a
> baton, which represents the gospel of Jesus Christ. At the
> appropriate moment, he hands the baton to you, and you
> begin your journey around the track. Then finally, the time
> will come when you must get the baton safely in the hands of
> your children.
>
> But as any track coach will testify, relay races are won or lost
> in the transfer of the baton. There is a critical moment when
> all can be lost by a fumble or miscalculation. If failure is to
> occur, it will probably happen in the exchange between gener-
> ations.
>
> My most important reason for living is to get the baton, the
> gospel, safely in the hands of my children and as many others
> as possible.

PRAYER

> Lord, we praise Thee for the good life and we praise Thee
> for the thorns. Help us understand that our trials are but bless-
> ings in disguise. Move us from praise to ministry, and O Lord,
> protect us from dropping the baton as we pass it to our chil-
> dren.

Questions for Chapter 13

1) Read several of the following Psalms and praise God for who He is: Ps. 9:1, Ps. 84:1-2, Ps. 104:33, Ps. 145:1-7. Now thank Him for what He has done.

2) Write a prayer below to express thanks to God for His presence and power during your life's journey.

3) How have you used the power of Jesus for ministry and service? Remember, "blessings should flow through you, not just to you!"

CHAPTER 14

My Second Journey

BRENNAN MANNING SUGGESTS in *The Ragamuffin Gospel* that many people between the ages of thirty and sixty—whatever their stature in the community and whatever their personal achievements— undergo what can truly be called a second journey.

A second journey can be precipitated by a variety of things. It can be an illness like mine, which reminds us anew of the inevitability of old age and death. It may be a businessman who is fired from his job or forced into early retirement by a new corporate executive. A friend of ours faced a second journey when he came home from a revival and found out his wife and children had moved out while he was away.

An eleven-car pileup when you are in car number four can initiate a new beginning. I was in such a wreck in 1984 and walked away with little more than a bruise from my seat belt and a run in my hose! A situation like that will cause you to value life and ask yourself *lots* of questions. Am I spending my time on the urgent or the important? Am I giving my life's energy to something that ultimately counts or is the energy of my life being wasted on trivia? Have I put off the call of God? Is my faith worth dying for?

As people congregated like vultures around me that eventful day, they all asked identical questions. First, they looked at *me* standing by my *totaled* vehicle, and said, "Is that your car?" I nodded, and then each one said, "The good Lord must have something He wants you to do!"

JOURNAL ENTRY

I read today about Jesus healing the blind man in Mark 8:22-26. Jesus touched him twice and verse 25 says, "He was

215

restored." I'm so glad You are still in the business of giving all
of us "a second touch."

Life's difficulties force us to break through the superficiality of
our lives to a deeper life within. Every time our life is given back to
us from such a trial, it is like a new beginning, and we learn better
how much it is worth, and make more of it for God and man.

I've concluded after reading my Bible that almost every human
has had experiences precipitating a second journey. Think about
Peter—his problems were the result of his own sin, but it can be
just as likely that we will have to live with the consequences of
someone else's choices. Virtually no one is exempt.

Second journeys are usually turnaround moments ushering people into a maximum revelation of integrity, strength, and character; the prelude to achievement. God sometimes takes away what
seems good to us, in order to give us the *best*. After all, the second
crop of roses is usually the best. Gloria Gaither, in *We Have This
Moment,* said, "We deal with reality at two points in our lives—birth
and death. If only we could always live our days with as clear a
vision of the things that matter as we do at those two times."

A. B. Simpson said, "Trials and hard places are needed to press
us forward, even as the furnace fires in the hold of that mighty ship
give force that moves the piston, drives the engine, and propels
that great vessel across the sea in the face of the winds and waves."

I've known since my teen-age years that God had a purpose for
my life, but believe me, an experience like that will give you a new
awareness of what really matters, what really counts. It is a shame it
usually takes a crisis in life to bring us back to an awareness of what
matters most. Second journeys usually end a life of "business as
usual" and begin a life of fresh purpose and new dreams.

JOURNAL ENTRY

"I know the plans I have for you," declares the Lord, "plans
to prosper you and not to harm you, plans to give you hope
and a future" (Jer. 29:11). Lord, give me a consciousness of
Your presence and just a "peek" into the larger life You have
for me. You see, no situation lies beyond the possibility of
redemption when God is in the picture.

I think our lives are full of tiny resurrections, whether it's a second chance to finish a forgotten task or simply finding a new way of serving God. At any time we can be reborn in some small way. Even in retirement, when we think the course is set, our lives can change.

Jonah experienced this—"Then the Word of the Lord came to Jonah a second time: 'Go to the great city of Nineveh and proclaim to it the message I give you.' Jonah obeyed the word of the Lord and went to Nineveh" (Jonah 3:1-3a NIV®).

What about you? What are you going to do with the rest of your life? Find a new assignment and get *busy*. You can't turn the clock back, but you can wind it up again! Life is like a great adventure only so long. Why waste a moment of it in a state of anxiety? Longfellow said, "Great is the art of beginning, but greater is the art of ending."

JOURNAL ENTRY

Help me remember "the purpose of life is not to avoid death" but to live fully and joyfully as long as I have breath to "declare Your works."

A second journey may be accompanied by a profound dissatisfaction with your present life. Are you tired of waste—of living beneath your potential, mired in mediocrity? Maybe you are in a job that no longer fascinates—and you are waking up to the fact that money no longer satisfies. Serious reflection summons us to a more mature faith.

Changes Require Stretching

Changed circumstances, for whatever reason, force change upon us. Adversity can strengthen a relationship, redirect a life, and provide hope and inspiration for all. Pain causes us to look beneath the surface, and it disrupts and reshapes. Life is eternal but everything else is temporal. However, that's not all bad.

One of the gifts of life is the changing of the weather and the seasons. As we relinquish some of our illusions of control, we realize that each change of the weather and each season of the year has many gifts in store for us, if we participate in them and live them. When we fight and struggle against the weather, we dissipate the energy that could be used for enjoying.

I experienced a traumatic change recently—at least it was for me. I ate Thanksgiving dinner *out*. Now I know people do that all the time, but not *me*. I had always said if I ever ate Thanksgiving or Christmas dinner out, you would know I was over the hill!

JOURNAL ENTRY

This week has been Landrum's sixty-fifth birthday, Roland and Lisa's tenth anniversary, and Thanksgiving. I did something I never thought I would do—I ate out on Thanksgiving! I'm so grateful David and Vicki are still around to cushion the loss of others being so far away. Help me accept the changes, moves, situations beyond my control with grace. We have been fortunate having our children close by for longer than most people do, and I know that, and I am grateful. Help me be flexible—and just maybe this is *Your* way of relieving stress for me.

The amazing thing I learned is, change isn't necessarily bad. I actually *enjoyed* the day out with family and friends.

The Christian life is a dynamic process, and growth sometimes means being stretched beyond your comfort zone. Maybe we ought to pray for:

Enough happiness to keep you sweet—
Enough trials to keep you strong—
Enough sorrow to keep you human—
Enough failure to keep you humble—
Enough hope to keep you happy—
Enough success to keep you eager—
Enough friends to give you comfort—
Enough wealth to meet your needs—
Enough enthusiasm to look forward—
Enough faith to banish depression—
Enough determination to make each day a better day
    than yesterday—

Enough faith and humility to keep you in the center of God's
will for your life.

Source Unknown

Why is it so hard to trust God with the changes? In spite of all my
experience at seeing Him meet my needs and provide adequately
for me, I *still* want to worry about the future. Isn't it amazing how
many good experiences we can have and still remain the same?

It encourages me that even the disciples, those closest to Jesus,
had the same problem. After seeing Him feed the 5,000 with five
loaves and two fishes, they should have believed *anything* was possible. Yet immediately following that incident we find them "afraid"
in the midst of a storm when Jesus came to them walking on the
water (see Mark 6:50-52).

The disciples should not have forgotten so easily . . . nor should
we in our crises. The Lord gives His present miracles, not only to
help us now, but to give us lively confidence for the future.

JOURNAL ENTRY

Just as I never dreamed I would be where I am today, I can
never imagine what the future holds. Help me tear into the
smallest pieces any itinerary I may have for the journey.
Nothing will fall out as I expect, I'm sure. If "His ways are higher," then it's got to be better than my imagination could draw
up! Angel Martinez preached recently on His *thoughts* are different, His *techniques* are different, and His *time* is different.

Psychiatry has suggested that one characteristic of a mature person is the ability to face one's death. We are on a journey *home.*
Death is inevitable, a natural part of the journey of life. We forget
we are always only a heartbeat away from total powerlessness. It is
like the fourth quarter of a ball game with no time-outs left.

The Psalmist warned us about life's transience when he wrote Ps.
103:15-16, "As for man, his days are as grass: as a flower of the field,
so he flourisheth. For the wind passeth over it, and it is gone; and
the place thereof shall know it no more." We plan as though we
can escape the inevitable and forget there is one death for every

person born. We prepare for everything else—why not the one absolutely certain event?

Ps. 146:4 says, "For every man must die. His breathing stops, life ends and in a moment all he planned for himself is ended" (TLB). The surest thing about life is that one day it will end.

How would you spend your time if you knew that this year would be your last on earth? Do you have unfinished business you would need to take care of? Would you search your heart for unworthy attitudes that need changing, or for wrong actions for which you need God's forgiveness? Would you be satisfied with your present life-style? Would you pray earnestly for assurance that you have a personal, saving relationship with Jesus Christ? Do you have friends or loved ones who need your witness if they are to be ready to meet the Lord? How about your service to God through His church?

Does your life right now reflect the preparedness necessary to leave it? Good question. It matters not what your personal beliefs are; you cannot alter the reality of heaven and hell. (See Matthew 18:1-9.) Eternity in heaven is open to all who meet God's conditions. Hell is for those who choose otherwise.

Scripture reminds us: "Remember now your Creator in the days of your youth, before the difficult days come" (Eccles. 12:1). It is never too early to receive Christ, but at any moment it could be too late. Regardless of age, we must prepare for the future.

There is an old fable that illustrates this truth. A man made an unusual agreement with Death. He told the Grim Reaper that he would willingly accompany him when it came time to die, but only on one condition—that Death would send a messenger well in advance to warn him.

Weeks melted into months, and months into years. One frigid winter evening, as the man sat thinking about all his possessions, Death suddenly entered the room and tapped him on the shoulder. Startled, the man cried out, "You're here so soon and without warning! I thought we had an agreement."

The reply came, "I've more than kept my part. You have received many messengers from me. Look in the mirror and you'll see." As he did so, Death whispered, "See your hair! It used to be full and black; it is now thin and white. Look at the way you turn your head as you listen to me, because you can't hear very well. See how close to the mirror you stand to see yourself clearly. Yes, through the years I've sent many messengers. Too bad you are not ready, but the time has come to leave."

You may have had many similar warnings. While there is still time, believe in the Lord Jesus Christ and be saved. Seek Him now before you are called to keep that inevitable date with Death.

". . . Now is the accepted time; behold, now is the day of salvation" (2 Cor. 6:2 NIV®). Joy is not a destination, nor is it an emotion to be sought. Joy really *is* in the journey as I become rightly related to the Lord Jesus Christ.

PRAYER

Teach us, Lord, to dwell not on fading sunsets, but renewing dawn. Help me, as the song says, give *"all* my future to you!"

Questions for Chapter 14

1) Have you ever experienced a "second journey"—a turnabout moment in your life? How has your life been affected?

2) What changes have taken place in your life recently? Think of the benefits of those changes and thank God.

3) Read Ps. 103:15-16. How would you spend your time if you knew that this would be your last day on earth? Write a prayer to God asking for guidance in your future.

Credits

p. 39: Nancy Pannell, *Being a Minister's Wife and Being Yourself* (Nashville: Broadman Press 1993) 125. All rights reserved. Used by permission.

pp 57-58: Marcia K. Hornok, "Antithesis of Psalm 23," *Discipleship Journal* 10, no. 6 (November/December 1993): 23. Used by permission.

p. 104: Dave and Jan Dravecky, *When You Can't Come Back* © 1992 by Dave & Jan Dravecky. Used by permission of Zondervan Publishing House.

pp. 113, 155-56: Max Lucado, *God Came Near: Chronicles of the Christ* (Sisters, Oreg.: Questar Publishers, Multnomah Books 1987). All rights reserved. Used by permission.

p. 152: Marijohn Wilkin, "I Have Returned," copyright 1974 Buckhorn Music Publishers. All rights reserved. Used by permission.

p. 190: *Times-Record News* (Wichita Falls, Tex.), Tuesday, September 25, 1990, by staff writer Robin Sussingham. Used by permission.

p. 199: Anita Bryant, *A New Day* (Nashville: Broadman Press 1992) 142. All rights reserved. Used by permission.

p. 203: The chorus of the song "Guard Your Heart," by John Mohr, copyright © 1989, BMG Song, Inc., ASCAP—Birdwing Music (ASCAP). All rights administered and reserved by BMG. Used by permission.

p. 208: The song "Let Others See Jesus in You," by B. B. McKinney,

224 JOY IN THE JOURNEY

is taken from the *Baptist Hymnal,* copyright © 1924, renewal 1952, Broadman Press. All rights reserved. Used by permission.

p. 212: Dr. James Dobson, *Dr. Dobson Answers Your Questions* © 1982. Used by permission of Tyndale House Publishers, Inc. All rights reserved.